Skills Success at Level 2

Skills Success at Level 2

Mary Ambler
DipRSA

MACMILLAN

First published 1990

Published by
MACMILLAN EDUCATION LTD
Houndmills, Basingstoke, Hampshire RG21 2XS
and London
Companies and representatives
throughout the world

Printed in Hong Kong

British Library Cataloguing in Publication Data
Ambler, Mary
    Skills success at level 2.
    1. Typing
    I. Title
    652.3

    ISBN 0–333–51427–0

The names and addresses etc. used in
this book are fictitious. Any resemblance
to actual occurrences is purely coincidental.

☐ CONTENTS

Letters—20 Tasks
Tasks include carbon copies, routing, envelopes, attention lines etc, circulars, tear-off slips, postdating, locating information. A variety of subject matter is used.

Memos—20 Tasks
Tasks include carbon copies, routing, envelopes, confidential lines etc, postdating, locating information. A variety of subject matter is used, in some cases referring to a task in, say, Section 1.

General, articles, reports etc—20 Tasks
Tasks include agenda, minutes, specifications, reports and various types of articles giving a wide range of subject matter.

General, notices, etc—20 Tasks
Tasks include a wide range of topics, mainly using display, including emphasis, line-spacing, spaces, insets.

Tables—20 Tasks
Tasks include various subjects. Horizontal and vertical ruling is used, as well as split columns, alterations and re-arrangements.

Forms—15 Tasks
Tasks are handwritten instructions necessary for the completion of a printed form (a blank form included for each task). Tasks include invoices, booking forms, order forms etc. The instructions are presented in a variety of ways and the information has to be selected for insertion on the form.

☐ ACKNOWLEDGEMENTS

I wish to record my thanks for all the support I have received during the preparation of this book, especially for the help, encouragement and understanding of my husband and family. I also wish to thank Stephen Small and his staff at Small Office Supplies Limited of Keighley for their advice and services provided.

☐ NOTES TO STUDENTS

General

The following are being tested in many of the tasks in all sections:

    insets, headings, numbered or lettered paragraphs, footnotes,

    leader dots, line spacing alterations, spaces of specified

    sizes and capitalisation.

You are also expected to find and correct inconsistencies in:

    punctuation (open OR full) and always use the same number of
    spaces after the same punctuation mark

    words OR figures and fractions

    symbols (eg 20% and 5% OR 20 per cent and 5 per cent)

    measurements (eg 30cm x 30cm OR 30 cm x 30 cm; 12' 6" x 6' 3"
    OR 12 ft 6 in x 6 ft 3 in)

    money (eg £3 and £6 OR £3.00 and £6.00)

    times (eg 3.30pm and 6pm OR 3.30 pm and 6 pm OR 1530 hours and
    1800 hours)

    paragraphing (blocked OR indented)

Always follow copy as to capitalisation - it doesn't matter what you
think should have an initial capital or which words should be typed
all in capitals - it is the writer who decides - FOLLOW COPY AND YOU
WILL BE CORRECT.

You may be asked to type in future dates - make sure you know what
the date is and also how many days there are in a month.

Abbreviations are used - check with the list given whether they
should be typed in full or not.

Words which are simply circled in the copy have something wrong with
them - grammatical, punctuation or spelling/typing errors.

    (A) amendment will be made. = An amendment will be made.

    The (girls) bag is blue. = The girl's bag is blue.

    The young men (is) on holiday. = The young men are on holiday.

    I have (recieved) it. = I have received it.

You may have to refer to another task to find information necessary to complete a task or perhaps the information is somewhere else in the same task.

Always read through a task before starting to type and make certain you follow all instructions given - there may be an instruction at the end of a task which refers to, say, a heading at the beginning of the task. Read carefully through a finished task before taking it out of the typewriter - it is easier to align and correct errors. Check with the copy when you are reading through to see if you have missed out any words or even paragraphs. Use a line guide to prevent omissions.

Section 1 - Letters

The aim of this section is to give you plenty of practice in typing letters of various styles. There are both formal and informal letters. You are expected to use a letterhead for each task with printed "Our ref" etc. You can, of course, type these in if you have no letterheads. The tasks cover a variety of topics.

You can choose your own style of layout, either block or semi-block, so long as you are consistent. The choice is yours - ask your Tutor for details. You may be used to typing some particular "house-style" - that's quite acceptable as long as you are consistent in layout and presentation. For example, always use the same line spacing for similar instances. Make sure to leave sufficient space for the signature of the person sending the letter.

Although no instruction is given in the tasks, you are expected to date all letters. You should also check to see if any enclosures are mentioned and, if so, give an indication in some way.

You may be used to typing carbon copies and indicating to whom they are being sent - as long as it is clear to whom which carbon copy is to go to, that is sufficient. An easy way to indicate the routing is to type the names on all copies and tick or underline one diff-erent name on each copy. Remember also to correct any errors on the carbon copies.

You will often be asked to type an envelope. If there is some instruction, eg CONFIDENTIAL, in the letter, this should of course be included on the envelope. What is the purpose of putting CONFIDENTIAL on the letter and not on the envelope!

Section 2 - Memos

Again in this section, many of the above points apply. Memos should be typed on Memo paper. Many of the tasks include carbon copies, routing and envelopes - see instructions given for Section 1.

Memos are often more informal than letters and a courtesy title (Mr or Mrs etc) is not always used - don't add a title but follow copy.

Section 3 - General

Various types of tasks are included in this section. You are often asked to leave spaces of a certain size or vary the line spacing.

It is very important to use the same capitalisation as shown - the writer of the material knows what he/she wants. You may be asked to change, say, a heading into spaced or closed capitals. Details may require insetting from the left margin for display purposes. Transpositions are often required. Check all instructions.

Section 4 - General

Again in this section, tasks include a wide variety of topics. Display of material is required and variations in line spacing and spaces left for photographs etc are used. You may be asked to emphasise part of the work - the easiest way is to type the details all in capitals and/or underlined, or use the emboldening facility if your typewriter has one - make sure the details stand out.

You are often asked to change a word(s) to another word(s) - make certain you change all instances of the word(s). There may be unfamiliar words included - if in doubt, check with a dictionary.

Section 5 - Tables

All the tasks in this section require ruling up - treat yourself to a good rule and ballpoint or fine-liner pen. When ruling up a table, use a surface where you have plenty of room and the surface should be smooth to avoid "bumps" in ruling. Keep the paper straight when ruling to avoid crooked lines. Always leave sufficient space for vertical lines - you should not rule a line close up to the words in a column. Always leave space before horizontal lines.

Always leave at least one clear line space after headings (this applies to all sections) - a £ sign above a column of figures is a heading. Material has often to be re-arranged according to instructions. A word or words may have to be changed to something else. Follow the display used or any instructions as to display.

Footnote signs often appear in the tables - if a number or letter is used as a sign, it should be raised slightly to avoid confusion. If it is not raised in the footnote, it will look like a numbered paragraph!

Section 6 - Forms

I have included a blank form for your use at the end of the book. The instructions for completing the forms are not always given in the same order as required on the form. Always read through the details and check with the form before typing. For instance, you may have to insert an address and often there is a special space for the post-code which would not be apparent if the form was in the typewriter.

Words have to be deleted - align your typewriter in the correct position and delete only the words necessary. Avoid typing through dotted lines or through boxes. Careful alignment is required. All details given are not always required on the form - if there is no space for something, don't include it. Forms usually require dating but NEVER sign the form.

ABBREVIATIONS AND CORRECTION SIGNS

&	and	ffly	faithfully	ref	reference
a/c	account	Fri	Friday	req	require
accom	accommodation			resp	responsible
ack	acknowledge	gntee	guarantee		
advert	advertisement			Sat	Saturday
altho'	although	hr	hour	sec	secretary
approx	approximate(ly)	hv	have	sep	separate
appt	appointment			Sept	September
asap	as soon as	immed	immediate(ly)	sh	shall
	possible	incon	inconvenience	shd	should
Ave	Avenue	info	information	sncly	sincerely
Aug	August			suff	sufficient
		Jan	January	Sun	Sunday
bel	believe			St	Street
bus	business	Ln	Lane		
				thro'	through
cat	catalogue	mfr	manufacturer	Thurs	Thursday
cd	could	Mon	Monday	Tues	Tuesday
co	company				
Cres	Crescent	necy	necessary	w	with
cttee	committee	Nov	November	wd	would
				Wed	Wednesday
Dec	December	Oct	October	wh	which
def	definite(ly)	opp	opportunity	wl	will
Dr	Dear/Drive				
		poss	possible	yr	your/year
exp	experience				
		Rd	road		
Feb	February	rec	receive		

Some abbreviations must be retained, eg Co, &, Ltd, Bros, PLC/plc
etc in the names of companies and abbreviations such as etc, eg, VAT,
uPVC, PAYE, etc. In some of the tasks an instruction is given to
retain all abbreviations, including those mentioned in the first list
above. This instruction must be followed.

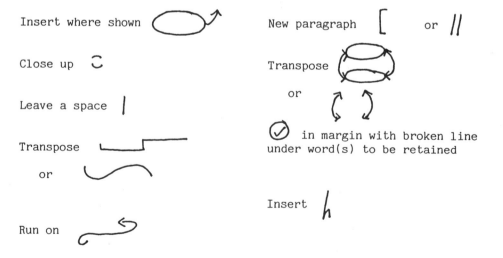

Insert where shown	New paragraph [or //
Close up	Transpose
Leave a space |	or
Transpose	in margin with broken line under word(s) to be retained
or	
	Insert
Run on	

If a word is simply circled with no instruction, there is something
wrong with that word - grammatical, spelling, typing or mis-agreement.

■ Section 1   Task 1 (approx 240 words)

Our ref 15.BM/pc

FOR THE ATTENTION OF MR C HUNTER

Quentin & Quentin Ltd
66 Leeds Rd
HUDDERSFIELD
West Yorkshire
HD6 6TR

2 carbon copies on yellow please – 1 for File and 1 for Glen Fawcett, Advertising

Dr Sirs

~~Solar Heating System~~ ← caps

                                                    increasing
In recent yrs there has been an/interest in solar energy because of the rising costs of traditional fuels.// Hundreds of homes are already using solar energy – why not offices? Solar power is free. By harnessing the Sun's power thro' a solar heating system you can ~~to~~ have energy even when there is no direct sunlight.

Selected
We now wish to install our SUNBEAM heating system in offices through~out the UK. If you wl assist us, we are prepared to install SUNBEAM in yr offices for a nominal ~~sum~~ amount. We wl bear the greater part of the costs. If yr co is interested in our project, please complete & return the enclosed Freepost card asap. ←

We will then visit yr offices & explain how our
caps → Sunbeam heating system will benefit yr co.

Yrs ffly

Brian Miller
SENIOR SALES EXECUTIVE

Envelope for addressee please

1

Please address the following letter to Mr and Mrs J Fanshaw
of 48 Carmona Lane, RINGWOOD, Hampshire, BH24 2RP.
Please type an envelope which should be marked FIRST CLASS.
Our ref is SA/fr.sp

Dear Mr and Mrs F_____

SCHOOL SPONSORED FUN RUN

As you ~~will be aware being~~ *are* Governors of the school you will
appreciate that we are very fortunate in having a mini-bus which
can be used by pupils for varied activities. It is, therefore,
essential that the school continues to have the use of a
reliable vehicle.

so many of the

The school is, in part, responsible for the upkeep and repair
of the mini-bus and for this reason we have to raise ~~money~~ funds.
The staff are organising and participating in a SPONSORED FUN RUN
to be held on Friday, *(date of Friday, next week please)* in
the school grounds.

Many pupils and parents will *also* be taking part in this event and it
is hoped that *(sponsers)* will lend their support. We are hoping to
raise £500. [I am writing to ask if you will be present at this
event to give your support ~~and to present awards~~. The Fun Run
will start at 1400 hours and refreshments will be provided in the
school hall.

for all between 3.30 pm and 4.30 pm

The school is able to participate in many types of field work, sport, visits and courses.

Please finish the letter → Yours sincerely

Stephen Armstead
Sports Master

TYPIST - please type this circular letter inserting month and year only. Our ref is PH/89/cd

(Please leave 6 clear line-spaces before salutation)

Dr Sir/Madam

The free one year gntee on yr Concorde appliance runs out next month. We are pleased to offer you the opp of extending yr gntee by taking out a fully comprehensive service contract. [An annual payment gntees a ~~speedy~~ service if you have a Concorde service contract. You wl have no (worryies) about repair bills. ⤵

(The service contract even covers (brakedowns) due to normal wear and tear, renewable until the product is 8 yrs old.

Simply ~~complete~~ (and return) the slip below it ✓ to us asap to make ~~sure~~ ~~certain~~ you are covered the moment yr present gntee expires. The annual payment is £✓. (leave space for 2 figures)

Yrs ffly

Peter Hunter
Contracts Department

- -

(Concorde Service Contract) ←caps

DOUBLE LINE-SPACING

Name --- - - - ... (64mm/2½")

Address _ _ _ _ _ — - _. (76mm/3")
_ _ _ _ _ _ _ _ _ . (")
_ _ _ _ _ _ _ _ . (")

Type of Equipment _ _ _ _ _ _ _ - (64mm/2½")

Model Number _ _ _ _ _ _ _ _ (20mm/¾")   Serial Number _ _ _ _ _ _ (20mm/¾")

I enclose £

Signature (38mm/1½") _ _ _ _ _ _   Date (38mm/1½") _ _ _ _ _ _

TYPIST - please type dotted lines at least the ~~lengths~~ indicated in brackets

3

Our ref KND/23-P
Mr. W. Heptonstall
48 Cliffe Ave
WEY MOUTH, Dorset.
DT4 8BF

> 2 copies on yellow please -
> one for file and one for
> Renewal Section. Please
> type an envelope to the
> addressee.

Dr Sir

> all letters and figures
> close up here

<u>Caravan Insurance</u> - Policy Number AZ 1614 BC 23

I refer to yr recently submitted proposal & now
have pleasure in enclosing the official Policy document
for safe-keeping. I thank you for allowing me
to arrange cover on yr behalf. [If, after perusal
of the document, you have any queries or ~~require~~
~~need~~ clarification of any point, please do not
hesitate to contact me.

One point I shd like to mention is that the
insurers issued the policy with personnel
belongings insured for the sum of £850. I am
obtaining their endorsement amending this to
£950, as stated on your proposal form. // Please
do bear in mind that my co deals w all types
of insurance including LIFE, PENSIONS and HOUSEHOLD
and the co enjoys favourable dispositions for the
placing of MORTGAGES.

I shall be glad to offer advise & quotations upon request.
Yrs ffly   (Leave space for signature)
K N Dranton ACIS
KEITH N DRANTON (INSURANCE CONSULTANTS) LTD

Our ref jg.subs/2

Mr. B. Medford,
27 Willow St.,
BUXTON,
Derbyshire
SK17 8EL

(Typist) - please type 2 envelopes, one for the addressee and one for Subscription department. Please mark letter and envelopes CONFIDENTIAL

Dear Mr M — — — .

(Subscription) - caps

for your attention,

I enclose, an 'Overdue Account' in respect of your subscription to

the Society.   Please send your payment as soon as possible, but

at the latest by Wednesday of next week, *(date please)*   .   [If

you have recently forwarded your payment, please ignore

this reminder.   If, how ever, you sent your payment some ~~while~~ *time* ago,

please *(advice)* our subscription Department in order that ~~enquiries~~

investigations can be undertaken.

We did have problems with the postage of invoices which were

sent with the last newsletter.   Please accept my *(apologys)* if this

is, in fact, the first account *you have recd.*

Please return the *('O/A') -in full* with your payment.

||I look forward to hearing of yr continued membership of the Society & wd thank you for the interest & support you hv given the Society over the ~~last few~~ yrs.

Yrs sncly

Jane Greene
(Assistant Secretary) - caps

2 Carbon copies please - one on yellow and one on white - the white copy to be indicated for Subscription department. The yellow copy is for file.

Please type the following letter to
Miss G. H. Bayley, 16 Castle Hill Rd, FISHGUARD,
Dyfed SA33 9PL

Dr Miss Bayley
Following our conversation at the last meeting
of the Photographic Club, I now enclose the leaflet, (Title
please - See Section 4. Task1), which I hope you wl
find ~~helpful useful~~. // I also enclose a copy of
our present syllabus & I look forward to seeing
you at some of the meetings. Please note the
following amendments to the list of secretaries:
(1) (Syllabus sec) - Mr Alan Cook, 35 William St,
        FISHGUARD, Dyfed, SA24 4PW
(2) (Print sec) - Mrs Eileen Morris, 8 Rowan Ave,
        FISHGUARD, Dyfed, SA18 3EF

Competitions are open to members only. If you are
thinking of entering any of the (Clubs') competitions,
it would be (adviseable) to become a member
asap.
Entries for the first major competition wl be
collected during the last week of next month.

Yrs Sncly

Stephen Maddock

An envelope for
Miss Bayley
please

6

Ref RJD/cara.WW

Mr and Mrs D Godfrey
26 Fairweather Cres
Hoole
CHESTER, Cheshire
CH19 7EL

Dr Mr and Mrs G——

Holiday Caravans

I write w ref to yr recent letter and have pleasure in enclosing our holiday pamphlet, (Please insert title - Section 3, Task 4). WEST WINDS HOLIDAY ESTATE.

We have vacances at the moment for the majority of the summer months but bookings are being made all the time and I wd advise early early application to avoid disapointment.

You stated in yr letter that you wd like a holiday in the Devon/Cornwall area of the country. West Winds is in an ideal position for a touring holiday of this area. You wl see from the pamphlet the facilities available at W— W—.

The tariff for our caravans vary slightly from month to month and so the details are listed below.

Inset by 12 spaces

May	£90
June	£94.50
July	£98.00
Aug	£115
Sept	£94.50

I also enclose a booking form for yr use.

Yrs sncly

Rachel J Dawson
Assistant Manageress

TYPIST - 2 carbon copies please on yellow - 1 for File and 1 for Bookings

PLEASE TYPE AN ENVELOPE FOR Mr and Mrs G——

Our ref GK.bc

Date with month and year only

Please leave 7 clear line-spaces here

Dear Sir/Madam

Are you thinking of moving ~~home~~ **house** in the near future. As estate (estate) agents with four offices in your area, we are aware of the demand for properties such as yours. We have a long list of prospective purchasers seeking new homes, like yours, in this area. (we) are sure that with the completion of the new ~~motorway~~ this demand will continue.
~~road network~~

Our valuation service is |entirely free| and |without obligation.| For an up-to-date valuation of your property, all you need do is ~~to~~ let us know when it will be ~~best~~ *convenient* for our valuer to call.

Call us now - our offices are **open 7 days a week from 9am to 5pm (Mon to Fri) and from 10.00am to 3.30pm (Sat and Sun).**

Double line-spacing for this para please

Yrs ffly

George Kitson

(G Kitson & Co Ltd) caps

As our 4 offices in this area are open for business every day they wl provide maximum market exposure. If you instruct us to put yr house on the market, we wl provide a speedy and efficient service.

Please insert as final paragraph

Please address this letter to Mrs M. McIntyre of Eversleigh, 91 Hope Cres, FOLKESTONE, Kent, CT18 3EL. Our ref is 684898710-FA/mj

Dr Mrs McIntyre

Thank you very much for replying to our letter & returning yr lucky numbers for our £75,000 'Mammoth Prize Draw'. [Yr own copy of our latest catalogue was sent to you immed. No doubt you have recd it by now. You wsl see that it is fully of superb fashions for you & yr family.

There is also yr free gift, Mrs Mc ——. This gift is reserved just for you & wsl be sent to you w yr first order. It is easy to place orders an order and you are sure certain to discover the advantages of shopping from our cat.

1   Marvellous choice - almost 1,300 pages of high-quality goods
2   7-day home approval
3   Payment is easy - up to forty weeks free credit
4   (Commision) - 10 per cent in goods or 8% in cash

I am certain that you wsl want to place yr first order asap, especially as yr first purchase entitles you to a free gift.

Yrs sncly

Frances Armitage

PS Good luck w yr numbers in the 'Mammoth Prize Draw' - Someone has to win - it could be YOU!

PLEASE LEAVE 4 CLEAR LINE-SPACES AFTER DATE

Dear Customer

                        personalised
Let me tell you about our stationery. Can you imagine your
own letterhead printed on high quality notepaper? The
notepaper is slightly translucant and it is a pleasure to
write on it. The printed letterhead has a raised texture and
is similar to embossing.

If you are not delighted with your order, simply return it to
us and we will refund your money.
               regarding
Details of ordering can be found on the order form enclosed. Simply
complete this and your order will arrive within 28 days, in a
presentation box.

Yrs ffly

J Wood
Wood (Stationers) Ltd

- -

*If you wish to see a sample of our notepaper, please
fill in this slip and return it to us at the above address*

Name ....

Address ....

        ....

        ....

*PLEASE TYPE IN DOUBLE LINE
SPACING AND MAKE EACH DOTTED
LINE AT LEAST 76MM (3")*

*Packs of stationary consist of either 100 A5
sheets w fifty envelopes for only £4·95, plus
£1·05 postage and packing, or the same
quantity in A4 size for £9·75, plus £1·25
p—— and p——.*

TYPIST - please type the following letter to Mr Kevin Jackson of
31 Windmill Avenue, SOUTHWOLD, Suffolk, IP18 8PG. Our reference
is GW/MA.sale

PLEASE MARK CONFIDENTIAL & TYPE AN ENVELOPE FOR MR JACKSON

Dear Sir

May I thank you for your kind instructions to act on your behalf in
respect of the sale of the above property.

Our comission will be based on the purchase price and will be
1% of the first £15,000 & 1½ percent of the remainder, plus £55
for 'set up' costs.

caps

A no sale, no charge agreement will come into operation 14 weeks
after the date of your instruction.

If the property is withdrawn from the market during this period
by the vendor, a charge of £55 will be made for out-of-pocket
expenses. If, however, the property is withdrawn after 14
weeks before a purchaser is found, there will be no charge.

Yours faithfully

The latter includes sale board, colour photography, all administration costs and a display of yr property in our offices. VAT will be added to the final costs.

Godfrey Watson
WATSON, SON & CO LTD

SALE OF 31 WINDMILL AVENUE

Please insert the following as the last paragraph -

The property wil be placed on the open market & an asking price of £49,500 wil be quoted. It wil be arranged for a sale board to be erected at the property.

2 copies please on yellow - 1 for File and 1 for Advertising Section

Your ref is GL.tg

Our ref TB/SA   Addressees - Messrs Lane, Walsh & Co
of 22 Main St, DAWLISH, Devon, EX18 6PT
Dr Sirs

We are opening new/offices in yr area after the
formation of a new co.

We wl be able to give you the best possible
(independant) advice. ||The co is very pleased
to have the services of Alan King, who wl
be Sales Director. Alan has both exp &
qualifications and all clients wl rec the best
guidance.

possible

The advantages of our advice (is) —

PLEASE
INSET BY
10 SPACES
AND LEAVE
A CLEAR
LINE-SPACE
WHERE *

We are free to deal with any co.
*
We are able to sell products on the
open market.
*
There is an unlimited choice of
products.

An experienced staff wl deal w pensions,
savings plans, life assurance cover, mortgages,
private medical insurance & investment plans.

All financial advice will be given to clients
in the strictest confidence.
↑ caps

Yrs ffly

Trevor Buckley
T & C Buckley & Co Ltd

Please mark FOR THE
ATTENTION OF MR G LANE
and type an envelope for
the addressee

Please mark CONFIDENTIAL

Your ref JM/bd   Our ref BH/AS/sem

To Miss M Miles, Seminar Secretary, Hill Bros PLC, Forest Rd, NOTTINGHAM, NG2 7EL

Dear Miss Miles

I write w ref to our telephone conversation of /last week. I can now confirm that the Headlands Hotel can accommodate yr (Companys) Sales Seminar next month. // I have ~~also~~ made a def ✓ booking ~~for~~ of the Yorkshire Suite. I understand that only sixty delegates will require overnight accom but that 95 delegates wl be attending the Seminar.

I enclose our buffet/ menu & perhaps you wl let me know the approx number requiring a buffet lunch by Fri of next week, (Date please). ←

(Lunch wl be served between 1230 hours and 2pm.

I also enclose a guide to our city & leaflets giving information on places of interest in the ~~region~~ area.

Yrs sncly

Bernard Hill
Seminar ~~Organise~~ Organiser

2 carbon copies on yellow - 1 for File and 1 for Restaurant

Please type an envelope to Miss M —

PLEASE TYPE THE FOLLOWING LETTER TO Mr S Mathers of 56

Windermere Crescent, Hipperholme, HALIFAX, West Yorkshire,

HX3 5TR.   Our reference is KT.ma/est

Envelope for the addressee please

Dear Sir

We thank you for your enquiry and /now have pleasure in
estimating as follows:-

PLEASE INSET THESE ITEMS BY 6 SPACES

* To supplying and fitting 4 white uPVC windows & 1 white uPVC door.

* All windows to be /fully welded and totally reinforced w box section aluminium. All openers to have adjustable multi-point sealing cams, key locking handles & ventilation keeps.

* Frames to be fully double glazed w 24mm sealed units.

* The door to have a 5-point locking system w locking latch and security dead bolt, hung on 4 die cast hinges.

* Total price including VAT - £1,734.21

*

We hope the above meets with /yr approval and await your further
instructions. If possible, please get in touch by Monday of next
week, (date please)   , before the start of the (firms)
holiday break.

Yrs ffly
HALIFAX GLAZING LTD

PLEASE LEAVE 2 CLEAR LINE SPACES WHERE * IS MARKED

(Keith Thompson) — caps

TYPIST - please type this letter to Mr J Owens, 78 Lane End
~~Avenue~~ **Rd**, MORECAMBE, Lancashire, LA3 9PD.   Address an envelope

to Mr Owens please, and also one to Personnel which should be

marked BY HAND

2 copies please - one to be marked for Personnel. Both copies on yellow please

Dear Sir

Share Option Scheme *caps*

Following the exercise of your "A" Option, I now enclose ~~herewith~~
your Certificate for 300 shares. // You will be entitled to
receive dividends on Ordinary Shares and to vote at any
shareholder's meeting. *) as a shareholder,*

The market price of Ordinary Shares on the date on which you
exercised your Option was 395p.

Any tax liability arising from the Option will be assessed at
the end of this *tax* year and dealt with as follows:

(1)   if you are liable to tax at basic rate, any tax wl be deducted thro' the PAYE coding system;

(2)   if you are liable to tax at a higher rate, tax will be
      deducted through the PAYE coding system if it amounts
      to less than £300, but, if more, it will be payble
      within 28 days.

~~Please do not hesitate to get in touch with me if you have any
questions on the above.~~

*If you have any queries about any of the above points, please contact
me at my office. Please note that I will not be there
until Thursday, (date of Thurs. of next week).*

Yrs ffly

M. Jowett *- caps*
Share Options Manager

Our ref EM.SE/6/6

Mrs M Fawthrop
"Loughrigg"
12 Church Ln
SPALDING, Lincolnshire
PE12 8BG

Envelope for Mrs Fawthrop please

Dr Madam

Our co are now recommending an inter-mediate service on all cars at six months or 6,000 miles, whichever is the sooner.

If, however, you have ommited to have this service, we can offer a 12 month service (12,000 miles).

The intermediate service includes an oil & filter change, plus an electronic tune, as well as all safety checks on yr vehicle.

The price of the 6 month service is £38.95, inclusive of parts & VAT. In addition, we are now able to offer a 12 month service, for a limited period, at £58.95, inclusive.

If you wish to take up our offer as out-lined above, please contact our service reception to make an appt. [Our co believes that all customers shd obtain maximum performance from a vehicle & therefore we are giving all customers the opp of this service offer.

Contact us asap and make an appt. ✗caps

Yrs ffly
BRIAR MOTORS LIMITED

Edward Moss
Service Engineer

16

Our ref DH/cth

(Please leave 5 clear line-spaces after date)

Dear Parent

Our fifth Annual Car Treasure Hunt takes place on Sat of next week, (Date?), and it is not too late to register. All you need do to compete for the Hunt Trophy (and/also for the booby prize!) is to bring your passengers and car to the school car park ✓between 1800 hours and 1830 hours on the ~~evening~~ night of the Treasure Hunt. [In exchange for the entry fee of £1.50 per car, you wl be given instructions & clues, to the Hunt's mystery destination.] (for the route)

Supper wl be available in the school hall from 9pm until 10pm, so make ~~certain~~ sure you solve the clues & arrive back on time. Supper is a very reasonable 50p per person.

If you wish to compete, please ~~complete~~ fill in the registration slip & return it to school asap.

Yrs ffly

(David Holliday) — caps
Deputy Head

(broken line edge to edge of paper)
↓
- - - - - - - - - - - - - - - - - - - -

(Car Treasure Hunt) — caps

Please register my car as an entry for ~~to~~ the Treasure Hunt.

DOUBLE LINE SPACING PLEASE
Registration Number ....
Name ....
Parent of ....
Please indicate how many suppers may be reqd ....

(First and last dotted lines to be at least 25mm/1"
Second and third   ..   ..   76mm/3")

17

Letter from Jacqueline Ramshaw, Area Sales Supervisor
to Mr A K Bhangoo, Newsagent, Lindholme Rd, BRADFORD,
West Yorkshire, BD4 8PK.   Ref (our) JR.del/3

Dr Sir   *An envelope for the*
                                 addressee please

<u>Deliveries</u>

I refer to yr recent letter and I have been investigating
the matter of late deliveries of our newspaper on Fridays.
Apparently this is caused by the early rush hour & road
congestion in the city centre. [We suggest that on
Fridays you take the earlier edition of the news~paper
as this shd be delivered to you by 1330 hours at the
latest. ⟵

As you ~~are aware~~ know, the edition you are at present
having delivered does not leave our dispatch/point until
3.30pm at the earliest.

As an alternative, I wd be prepared to re/route the
delivery van for a trial period of 3 weeks w the
intention of over~coming traffic ~~problems~~ congestion in
the area.

All correspondence regarding this matter shd be addressed
to Mrs Postlethwaite, Dispatch Office.

Will you please inform our Dispatch Office in writing if you
wish to rec the earlier edition. ~~If oth~~ If we do not
hear from you by Thurs of next week, (Date please), it
wl be arranged for the re-routing of the delivery
van.

Yrs ffly etc   *2 copies please —on yellow—*
     (see above)   *1 for File and 1 for*
                            Mrs Postlethwaite, Dispatch Office

Please use same Ref and name of sender and designation as used in Task 5 of this Section

Please leave 4 clear line-spaces after the date

Dear Member

Overdue Accounts

outstanding

Last month we sent "Overdue Accounts" to members having ~~a~~ payment on their subscription.

We have recd complaints as follows:

investigating

1   RECORDING OF PAYMENTS   We are ~~looking into the matter of~~ payments alleged to have been made and not recorded with the accounts department.   Members will be advised if payments have been (recieved.)   *asap*

type like this

2   (Window Envelopes)   Our mailing department unfortunately used the incorrect window envelopes ~~resulting~~ in the red "Overdue Account" lettering appearing in the envelope window.

which resulted

Yours faithfully

Please insert the numbered paragraphs 5 spaces

||Insert the following as a final paragraph - ||

We wish to apologise for any (embarasment) caused to members as a result of the above and more attention wil be given to the recording of payments and envelope use in the future.

2 copies please on yellow - 1 for ACCOUNTS DEPARTMENT and 1 for MAILING DEPARTMENT

Section 1   Task 20 (approx 270 words)

PLEASE TYPE THIS LETTER TO Miss J Raja, 15 Hill Avenue,
BAKEWELL, Derbyshire, DE4 8PW.   Use PH/WP as the
reference.

Dear Miss Raja

Word Processing Courses ← caps

I refer to your recent telephone call to my department evening
and I set out below details of our word processing courses
to be held during this college year.

(a) WP/1a - a course for beginners for which no qualifications are necy. Classes are held twice a week, on Mons & Weds from 6pm to 8pm. There is a college examination at the end of the course.

(b) WP/2 - a course for students w a knowledge of word processing & a typing skill to a standard equivalent to RSA stage 1. Classes are held once a week on Thursdays from 6.30pm to 9pm. There is an external examination at the end of the course.

(c) WP/1b - a course for students with a stage 1 certificate in w— p—. Classes are held twice a week on Mons & Thursdays from 1800 hours to 2000 hours. There is an external examination at the end of the course.

There are also some part-time day courses, but if you require
details of these, please give me a ring (601284 extension 32.

Enrolments will be taking place on Mon & Tues of next week,
dates please   , in the main hall of the
college campus.

Yours sincerely

Patricia Humphries
WORD PROCESSING TUTOR

☐ SECTION 2 — MEMOS

■ Section 2   Task 1 (approx 190 words)

Memo to Ann Falls, Catering from John Binns,
Training   Ref TD.hc/1

2 carbon copies on yellow – 1 for File & 1 for Personnel

Hygiene Course

The following employees will be attending a Hygiene Course to
be held next week, on *Thurs, (date?)*,   in the lecture
hall at head office.

All course members will need require lunch which will be at
approx 12.30 pm   in the main dining hall. Coffee
will be served in the morning at 10.30 am and tea in the
afternoon at 1500 hours.   .

*No doubt you wl see to the seating
arrangments but perhaps you wd let me have
a copy of the menu alternatives asap. ⑤
⑥ I wl then let you know the menu
requirements by Tues at the latest.*

*Mr B Bradford   Mrs S Box   Ms M P Cowell
Mr S T Fielding   Mr C Greene
Ms V Hartley   Mr A S Lee   Mr J V Longden
Mr T J Neale   Ms B Oates   Mr R P Peake
Mr K Pemrose   Mr J K Riddiough
Mrs. L. Stringfellow   Mrs. P. Swift   Mr P Sykes
Miss S. Weatherhead*

↑

*PLEASE INSERT THE ABOVE NAMES
AFTER THE FIRST PARAGRAPH, IN
ONE COLUMN AND INSET 6 SPACES
USE THE SAME ORDER READING FROM
LEFT TO RIGHT.*

(Memo)

From Chief Engineer to Maintenance
Supervisor   Ref - CE/MA/m

(Factory Stoppage) ←caps

Since the meeting ᵒⁿ last Mon between ᵗʰᵉ management
and the union, there has been very
little progress towards ending the dispute. ⤶

Both sides (is) working separately on a
solution formula & are prepared to meet
at quick notice if either side has a
proposition.

As the factory closes on Fri in a
(fortnights) time, the Holiday work wl
commence & the maintenance department
wl be working the hrs that have
~~already~~ already been agreed for this work.

The maintenance department must only
attempt jobs that can confidently be
~~finished~~ completed within twenty-four
hrs. Until further notice this strategy
wl continue & if the strike continues
next week there is suff work for
the department for 39 hrs.

(PLEASE MARK CONFIDENTIAL)

This memo is from Peter Sykes, Site Manager to John Newby,
Works Manager. The reference is PS.pl.8

Following the ~above~ meeting held last Thursday, I set out below
my report on ~the~ progress of the new building.

1. ~A~ try attempt was made to replumb the columns supporting the
   outer edge of the gantry.

2. Glazing installation commenced but work stopped ~due to because
   of~ cills not having a forked return end. This work is to
   re-commence on Monday, (date - Mon of next week).

3. The partition system is still in progress with an anticipated
   completion in a (fortnights) time.

5. A steel staircase to the gantry has been installed.

4. Automatic rubber doors (has) been installed but one door ~newel~
   post is twisted. The covers over the door closer mechanism are
   yet to be removed.

6. Arrangements have been made for a
   stainless steel balustrade to be fixed
   to the staircase in sections to
   facilitate easy removal.

Please let me know if you have any comments
on the above.

I will be arranging the next Site Meeting
on a date yet to be agreed with the
Architects but I hope it will be in the
first week of next month.

TYPIST - Please insert Site Meeting 8 as a heading
  - 2 copies please on yellow - 1 for File and
    1 for Mr Philip Jackson
  - Please type an envelope for Mr Philip
    Jackson, John Mathers & Partners,
    Architects, BINGLEY. West Yorkshire, BD16 6EL

Ref io TA.154/ac   From Tess Allen to John Logan

Pass book - Norman Wallace — caps

I enclose the above passbook (526 905 2033) and sh be obliged if you wl audit the same and confirm that the balance agrees w the computor records. [This passbook has been at the office for some time now and I ask that you deal w this matter asap.

The problem in the records appear to be in the period 15 June to 15 Sept.

Please return the passbook to me in order that I may return it to the holder.

Please mark CONFIDENTIAL and also type an envelope to John Logan, Accounts Department

TO Staffing Manager

FROM Finance Director

DATE

REF F/DP/sal

Salaries - Part-time Employees   ~ caps

part-time

It has come to my attention ~~notice~~ that, as of late claim forms
from employees are being sent to the payroll section too
late to be included in the computer proceses for payroll.

There is also what seems to be a growing practise of making
single ~~entries~~ submissions of claims for a multiple of periods.

I do realise that you are reliant upon these Employees submitting
claim forms on time but it is now becoming intolerable and
payroll in future will not make payments for late claims.
Employees will have to wait until the claim period for next
payment.

stress

I would appreciate it if you could ~~make clear~~ the importance of
submitting claims on time and in respect of the appropriate
period.

The above puts additional workloads on payroll as individual calculations have to be made.

2 carbon copies please on yellow —
1 for FILE & 1 for PAYROLL SECTION

25

Memo to Keith Jones, Personnel from Jim Picknall, Sales
Ref JP.ma/ad

Advertisement - Vacant Post

(draft) With reference to your telephone call yesterday, I now give
below an advertisement for the post of Regional Sales
Office Controller.

↕ (Leave 3 clear line-spaces) (Northern)

* Following reorganisation at the Regional Sales Office, there
is a vacancy for a ~~Regional~~ Sales Office Controller.

(and system resources)

* The (sucessful) applicant will be responsible for the
effective use of personnel within the Sales Office. There
will be involvement in |operational| and |commercial| decisions
in the development of sales and administration practices.

* The appointment is likely to suit a person with ~~knowledge~~
~~and~~ experience as a supervisor and with a knowledge of
computer/word processing operations and office automation.

↕ (Leave 3 clear line-spaces here)

I have not included the grade and
application details and, no doubt,
you wl add this necy info to the
final copy. || Will you please insert
this advert in the relevant
newspapers asap.

(TYPIST - please inset the paragraphs
marked * by 5 spaces)

26

Section 2   Task 7 (approx 230 words)

To   Richards Roberts   Date

From Samantha Greene   Ref RR|SA|21

SEMINAR ON DISCIPLINARY ACTION - FRIDAY (date, Fri of next week)

Will you please note that this Seminar will now be held in Conference
Room B and not Room D as originally planned.

I set out below the programme showing the times and topics.

```
0930      Introduction - Mr R Roberts
1000      Programme of Case Studies - Ms L Wilson      Please type this
1100      Coffee Break                                 section in
1115      Discipline at Work - Mr K Sutton             double line-spacing
1230      Buffet Lunch                                 and inset by
1315      Fact Investigation (Video)                   10 spaces
1400      Comments on Case Study - Mr R Roberts
1500      Interviewing (Video)
```

Morning coffee will be taken in the Conference Room but an
adjoining dining room will be made available for lunch. Afternoon
tea will be served during the (vidoe) at 1500 hours.

                             programme
Will you please arrange for the above to be photo copied and
sent to all (supervisers) who are attending the Seminar. I have
sent a copy of this note to Lucinda Wilson. Keith Sutton is on
holiday this week but no doubt you will let him know of the changes
on his return.   (room)

Please insert the following in the
correct places
    11.45 am Case Study
    3.30 pm   General Discussion

Please do 2 copies on yellow - 1 for
Lucinda Wilson and 1 for File

From   Head of Business Studies
To   All Staff, Business Studies
Ref   BS. ta/po

REGISTERS

The administration section ws̶l̶ b̶e̶ ~~having~~ conducting
a check on/registers next week. Will you please,
                  all
therefore, leave yr register in room 3A on
Wed, (next Wed's date please). Part-time staff
may leave registers ɯ the enrolment office
if room 3A is locked. You may collect yr
register on the following Fri. //Registers must
be/completed with names, enrolment numbers,
    fully
addresses and telephone numbers. The class number
(eg T/1/W) shd appear on the ˄cover. (front)

Please make ~~certain~~ sure all info is up-to-date. ⟲

(If any student has not attended class for more
than 2 (weeks') without any notice, his/her
name shd be withdrawn.

                                            to be
If you have any queries on information/included,
✓please ~~get in touch~~ ~~contact~~ with me.

┌───┐
│ TYPIST — 2 carbon copies please on yellow — 1 for
│ File ⅄ 1 for Administration section. 1
│ will arrange to have photocopies taken for
│ circulation.
└───┘

Memo from Roger Webster to All Heads of Sections
Ref - RW/GT/acc

(Accident Reporting) - caps

2 copies please on yellow -
1 for Sister Fairweather
1 for Reginald Walker

Will you please note the / ~~the~~ reporting procedures relating
^{new}

to the completion of the Report of an Accident at Work (RAW)

and the Privileged Information (PI) forms should commence

forthwith.

In all cases both RAW and PI forms, when completed, must be

sent to Sister Fairweather, simultaneously, not (seperately.)

It has been brought to my ~~attention~~ that a number of people
^{~~notice~~}

who may be called upon to complete these forms have not yet

attended the appropriate course by Reginald Walker,

Training Officer.

I enclose / the forms for your use.
^{a supply of}

Will you, therefore,
please arrange for
any such staff in
yr section to
contact Reginald
and arrange training asap.

Please ~~it~~ also note that the ~~supervisor/itt~~
supervisor/section head is resp when completing
the RAW form to detach the / section ~~at the foot~~
^{lower}
marked Report of Accident at Work Initial
Safety Representative Information and ~~for~~ forward
this section to the appropriate safety
representative.

PLEASE INSERT THE ABOVE AS THE SECOND
PARAGRAPH

Memo from Henry Osbourne to Joanne Ravell

Ref: HO/TG-ta

Please mark URGENT

<u>Travel and Accommodation</u>

Leeds/Bradford

I have just heard that I have to travel to East Anglia next week to view some premises in Felixstowe and Norwich. Will you please arrange a flight from the Airport to arrive in Norwich at the earliest poss time on Tues next week, date please.

I sh require accom at N— for 2 nights — bed, breakfast and evening meal. If at all poss will you try and book me in at the Crown Hotel — I have stayed there before and it is first-class. If the premises viewed are suitable, I wl contemplate extending my stay for a further three days. I sh be obliged, therefore, if you wl make a provisional booking for the extra nights. I wl be able to make a def booking on the Tuesday.

Please let me have the times of flight etc asap. I will make my own arrangements for the return journey.

I will also require the use of a hire car for the following day, date?, as I propose driving to Felixstowe and back on that day.

Section 2   Task 11 (approx 175 words)

To   Richard Watt, Development   Date

From   Stephen Hopkins, Maintenance   Ref   RW/b/ma

SPARES — *lower case & underline*

Further to the brief summary ~~sent to you~~ *provided* earlier, enclosed is a list of recommended spares. *from each of the mfrs involved*

Also

Enclosed are quotations from alternative sources where considerable savings can be made. Again items which general opinion felt we should stock are high lighted red. Spares which appear on typed lists are deemed necessary, *but shd be sourced elsewhere than the supplier.*

I have ~~checked~~ *been thro'* this list with Peter Thomas, Martyn Ross and, on some items, yourself, and the items which it is generally felt we should buy from the (supliers) are highlighted red.

Your judgement, of course, may be that spares over and above those highlighted shd be stocked; in wh case feel free to extend the list.

2 carbon copies please on yellow
1 for File and 1 for Stores

Please use single line-spacing

Memo from Rachel Thomas, Reception   to Stephen Wright, Publicity

Reference — RT/Rec/42   *   Please inset the list of leaflets required by 6 character spaces

L̲eaflets̲

The Reception Area requires /further information leaflets as follows:

*

MUSEUMS	100 of Pack 2
(Please type all these headings like this)	100 of Pack 4
	150 of Pack 5

ART GALLERIES   50 of Pack 1
                 50 of Pack 2

Walks   100 of Sheet 3   150 of Sheet 5
         150 of Sheet 8

Country Houses   100 of Sheet 3
                 150 of Sheet 4
                 100 of Sheet 8

Hotels   50
Restaurants 50
Tours   100

(of most)

Will you please let me have the above asap as we are almost out of stock of the leaflets & enquiries are being made daily. // I understand that new Walk Sheets 11 and 12 will be issued ~~soon~~ shortly & no doubt you wl let me have, say, 200 of each.

The following memo is to All Members of Staff from Headmaster Ref - Head/TA/232

(School Timetable) ←caps

With effect
~~As~~ from the beginning of next term, it is proposed to use the following time structure, resulting in the earlier finish of the school day.

(Morning)← underline →(Afternoon)

Morning	Afternoon
0850 Registration	1300 Registration
0900 Period 1	1310 Period 5
0945 Period 2	1350 Period 6
1040 Period 3	1430 Period 7
1125 Period 4	1510 End of school day
1210 Lunch	

If you have any suggestions or comments on this time table, please let me have them by Friday of next week, (please insert date).

think
I ~~do know~~ that the majority of parents ~~are~~ will be in agreement with the earlier finish, especially during the winter when it is often (months) dusk about 4 pm.

A copy of this memo has been sent to Alan Masters and a copy of the proposed timetable will be sent to all parents, via the pupils, inviting comments.

(10.30 am Break)

2 carbon copies please - 1 on White and 1 on Yellow. Route the white copy for Alan Masters, Area Education Officer. The yellow copy is for File. Please type an envelope to Mr Alan Masters, Area E — O — and mark ~~it~~ BY HAND

33

Ref BH/D5/sem   To Gary Fortune, Chef

From Bernard Hill, Seminar Organiser

SALES SEMINAR   (See Task 13 in Section 1)

I have now had confirmation from Miss Miles of H — B — P —
that sixty delegates will require overnight accom but 95
w/ be attending the seminar. A buffet lunch w/ be reqd
for 95 people on Thurs of next week, (please insert date).
I have booked the Yorkshire ~~Room~~ Suite for this
Seminar & I think it w/ be appropriate to use the
Harrogate Room for lunch. This room is ~~quite~~ capable of
holding 120 people for a buffet & is adjoining the Y — S —.
Please let me know if you think this room would __not__
be suitable. // The lunch is to be served between
1230 hrs and 2 pm. I sent a copy of our menu to
Miss Miles &I enclose her reply w (reference) to
requirements.
Please let me know if you have any difficulties in
meeting the menu requirements.

buffet

Memo to Peter Gamble from ~~Veronica Ware~~ Veronica Ware

Ref VW/pms (44)   MARK CONFIDENTIAL

Identity Cards ←—caps

It has been decided that a new style of identity card (are) to
be issued next month. All staff will be asked to produce an
existing card in exchange for a new one. Some members of staff
have said that the cards are too large for purses and wallets
and, therefore, the new cards will measure approximately 70 mm
by 45 mm. Photographs will measure 30mm by 30mm.

It has been brought to my (atention) that part-time and
temporary staff are not always aware of changes in systems.
Will you please ensure that (all) staff (recieve) a note, ~~telling~~
~~them~~ ~~about~~ the new identity cards.   giving info on

I enclose a sample of the wording to be used on the cards. I
                              receive
sh be pleased to ~~xxx~~ yr comments asap.

> TYPIST - please type a label for Stephen
>   Greenwood, Security
>
>   and mark CONFIDENTIAL

It wl be necy, as a result of the smaller
s8ize, for staff to have new photographs. ⟵
Arrangements are being made for the use of
the colour photograph machine by all staff
on Thurs and Fri of next week (dates please).

2 copies on yellow - 1 for File and
1 for Stephen Greenwood

caps

Memo to Eve Postlewaite   from Jacqueline
Ramshaw.   Ref   JR/SALES/mf

Deliveries

Please refer to TASK 18,
SECTION 1

I refer to my recent letter I sent to Mr AKB—,
Newsagent, L—R—, a copy of wh you recd. It
has been brought to my ~~attention~~ ~~notice~~ that
this Newsagency is in the process of being
sold. The new owners will be Mr and Mrs Prajapati.
// Will you please let me know if you have heard
from Mr B— with regards to deliveries as
I wish to amend my sales sheet as soon as
Mr and Mrs P— take over the shop. I
understand that this is likely to be at the
beginning of next month.
There ~~seems~~ appears to/ have been a few changes in
deliveries in the last few weeks and I sh be
obliged if you will let me have all details.
If we continue to rec complaints about
deliveries, we sh have to decide on the course
of action to be taken. Will you please keep a
check on complaints in the future. ←
I will, of course, let you know when I have
arranged a meeting to discuss this matter.

2 ccs on yellow – 1 for James
Halliday, Orders – 1 for File

TO   Mr S Preston   DATE today's date

FROM Mr W V Simpson   REF SP/345/KTH. rad fod

PLEASE MARK
URGENT

RADAR PT19

associated

✓ I enclose the documentation connected with the above radar system.
This consists of:

PLEASE
INSET   a copy of the system/test results;
BY 6
SPACES   form 845 - the master, which will require your signature, is
         still with Gareth Dinsdale;

         form 62 - this details the system performance short falls and
         also the build system standard shortfalls.

I would be grateful for your early consideration of these documents
so that if they are acceptable you can sign form 845. If you have
any queries, please contact Gareth Dinsdale. or myself

either

Following our normal procedure we have facsimiled
the concession to Anthony Blake. A copy of the
front sheet of the facsimile is also enclosed,
together with 3 xerox copies of the concession.

2 copies on yellow paper - 1 for
Miss M A Spooner and 1 for
Mr D Woodward.

To All Casual Car Users From Frank Nolson,
Treasurer's Department   Ref Treas/FN/JP

I have been advised by the local authority
that ~~as in the past~~ previous yrs the
Inland Revenue require details of all staff
who have used cars for business & have
travelled between 1600 and 2500 miles. [When
the (milage) returns for the current
financial yr have been assessed by
the Inland R — as to the receipt
⊘ of any provisional ~~profits~~ gains, yr tax code
for next yr will be amended accordingly.

The following shows the agreed provisional
profits, ie the profit element of the
mileage allowance which is paid.

Mileage	
500 - 1499	~~nil~~ nil
1500 - 2499	150
2500 - 3499	140
3500 - 4499	130
5500 - 6499	110
4500 - 5499	120
6500 - 7499	nil

to margin

These figures are based on cars w an engine
size of 1000cc - 1499cc. The figures for smaller or
larger cars vary slightly and if you require
these, please let me know.

Please head this memo TAXATION OF CAR
ALLOWANCES

Section 2   Task 19 (approx 200 words)

Please type a memo to Jamie McIntyre from Rachel McCallion.
The reference is RM/jw/pub

Corda Realm 1500 - Advertising Feature ← caps

The following is to be included in the advertising feature
of the new Corda Realm 1500.

↑ Please leave 3 clear line-spaces here

PLEASE TYPE IN DOUBLE LINE SPACING

The Corda Realm 1500 has a very sleek profile but has a practical
hatchback layout. It has been designed with maximum comfort,
space, economy and performance in mind.

The Corda Realm 1500 has front wheel drive and has a very efficient
in-line engine. The 5-speed manual transmission gives maximum
fuel consumption.

panels
Lightweight steel body further enhances economy and all
the bodywork is guaranteed against corrosion for 5 years.

↑ Please leave 3 clear line-spaces here
↓ already
You have seen the paragraphs on extras and safety. I have sent
a copy of this memorandum to the Advertising Section.

As there is a meeting on Friday of next week, (date?),
please let me have yr reply asap.

Will you please let me have yr views on the above
and make any alterations you think necy.

2 copies please on yellow - 1 for
ADVERTISING SECTION and 1 for FILE

(Memo)

From Personnel Officer,   Head Office
To Area Manager, Skegness Branch
Ref MR. Pers/SA

(Please mark
CONFIDENTIAL)

Staff Transfers

W ref to your request for /extra staff, the easiest solution to
this problem is to re-deploy 3 office staff from our Lincoln
/B Branch. All three are willing to work in Skegness - 1 is a
young single girl with no particular home ties & the
other 2 are both young /married men who are wishing to settle
down in near Skegness.

The names & addresses of the staff concerned are:-

Please
type in
double
line
spacing

MR G Farmer, 22 Oak Ln, Waddlington, Lincoln, LN5 8NR
MR H.J. Snow, 43 Barnham Rd Lincoln, LN5 8WR
Miss J Skelwith, Flat 5, 12 Stoney Rd, Lincoln, LN4 6TW

All 3 staff understand that once they have been re-deployed,
the opp to change Branches will not occur again.// Copies to /of
the Staff Records are enclosed in order that you may
have the opp to peruse them before we meet ~~next~~ on
Thursday, /of next week (Please insert date), to discuss this matter.

As I have a /very tight schedule to meet on Thursday, perhaps
you cd arrange for us to meet over lunch at, say the
Red Lion Hotel.

(Please type an envelope for Area Manager, S— B—)

40

Section 3 Task 1 (approx 270 words)

BOWPALL TIMBER & DAMP CO LTD

Specialists in Remedial Treatments

↑ (LEAVE 4 CLEAR LINE-SPACES)

(Inset 10 spaces please) S P E C I F I C A T I O N of work to be carried out at 61 Meadow Cres, SCARBOROUGH, North Yorkshire, SC18 4PW, for and on behalf of Mr and Mrs N McIntyre of 23 Waterside Ave, SCARBOROUGH, North Yorkshire, SC12 3HN.

DAMP TREATMENT ← (Typist - the following 3 headings to be like this please)

The affected area/plaster to be chipped off to a minimum of 18" above any damp stains. Skirting boards, if in sound condition, to be removed carefully and/re-used (a further charge for materials only if new boards have to be provided). All joints to be raked out.

Injection

✓ This is to be done by drilling neat/holes at a ~~predetermined~~ level and injected by high (presure) with a silicone fluid. All holes, internal and external, to be filled with |cement| and |sand| mix and finished off.

Replastering

Apply backing of cement render w a water-proofing agent. Each coat of plaster to be finished off at no more than 3/8 inch thickness. A finish coat to be used of a preservation plaster. All plaster works to finish at 1" above floor level (if solid floor).

Wood Treatment

All new joints to have capped ends and treated with a bituminous compound. Any existing timber to be treated w a fungicidal fluid. Any plaster work affected by dry rot etc to be also treated in a similar way.

↑ (LEAVE 4 CLEAR LINE-SPACES)

(Today's date)

BILLS OF QUANTITIES — spaced caps   double line-spacing please
for
ALTERATIONS TO GREEN FACTORY
at
RIVERSIDE MILLS, BENTLEY STREET, BURNLEY
for
J & R AMBLER LTD

↑ leave 3 clear line-spaces here

BILL 1 - PRELIMINARIES

Employer ← The following 3 headings like this please

                                              st
J & R Ambler Ltd, Riverside Mills, Bentley ~~Road~~, BURNLEY.

SURVEYOR

Messrs Riddiough, Pellow and Gelder, Frank Street Chambers, BURNLEY.

ARCHITECT

Trent & Darby Ltd, Crown Buildings, Main St, BLACKBURN.

ENGINEER

Placo Designs Ltd, Manor House, Lord Street, BURNLEY.

existing
Description of Work

The works comprise the extension of the existing mezzanine floor
within the factory.

                                                    existing
The new mezzanine floor is to be built on the ~~present~~ upper level
of the factory.   The construction is as follows:-

The work is to be carried out whilst the factory is occupied and
must not restrict the working operations.
          in any way,
The programming of the work is to be carried out after consultations
with the Employer and Architect.

Steel frame and pre-cast concrete upper floor,
reinforced concrete and metal staircase, block
walls, with some floor and wall finishes.
                        ↑
PLEASE INSERT WHERE SHOWN
BUT INSET BY 10 SPACES

DOUBLE LINE-SPACING

caps

PLEASE INSET 3 SPACES

(Specification) of work to be carried out at 26 Newlands Park Avenue, EASTBOURNE, Sussex, BN18 4PW, for Mr James McCallion, to the satisfaction of Messrs B & G White, Fountain Hill, EASTBOURNE, Sussex, BN3 2CK.

⇧ (3 clear line-spaces here)
Today's date please

GENERAL	All materials and workmanship to be the best and all work to be carefully undertaken. ↩
	All rubbish etc to be cleared away and all rooms left clean and tidy.
DINING ROOM	One wall to be completely replastered. Plaster any cracks and finish off. Burn off paint from windows (amd) doors. Paper the ceiling and walls with wallpaper specified. Paint all woodwork with undercoat and 2 coats of white finish. (gloss)

MASTER BEDROOM

Strip off old paper and prepare all paintwork. Put in new wardrobe with mirror doors. Repaper ceiling and walls with specified wallpaper. Paint all woodwork with undercoat and two coats of white gloss finish. Existing wardrobe and chest of drawers to be disposed of.

LOUNGE

where necy
Prepare walls and ceiling and plaster. Burn off paint from doors and windows. Paper the ceiling and walls with best quality embossed wallpaper specified. Paint ceiling and walls with 2 coats of silk finish in the colour chosen by Mr McCallion. Burn off paint from doors and windows. Paint all woodwork with undercoat and two coats of white gloss finish.

BATHROOM
Remove bathroom suite completely. Remove all tiles from walls. Prepare and plaster where necy in readiness for tiling. Fit new 4-piece suite and re-tile all walls. Fix new shower unit.

TYPIST - please type the last 3 paragraphs in the same style as the GENERAL and DINING ROOM paragraphs.

WEST WINDS HOLIDAY ESTATE

an old manor house

West Winds Holiday Estate is set in the grounds of West Winds House. The estate covers approx 18 acres of grassland and woodland in a quiet and secluded ~~soth~~ south-facing valley. The nearest main town – Newquay – is only 3 miles away.

There is a regular bus service to the town and the bus stop is only a short distance from the entrance to the estate.

West Winds offers /all/ the amenities expected of a first-class holiday estate. There is a small self-service mini-market open all day and a cafeteria (including take away food service). There is a laundry w tumble driers and ironing facilities. An outdoor /swimming/ pool w sep (childrens) pool is available free of charge to all estate campers.

There are plenty of beaches within easy reach & Newquay has good shops, eating houses and ✓ entertainment facilities. ~~In addition to~~ /As well as/ the well-stocked estate shop, the local village can easily supply you w basic necessities.

↑ (LEAVE 4 CLEAR LINE-SPACES)

PLEASE TYPE IN DOUBLE-LINE SPACING

West Winds is ideally positioned /as a centre/ for touring Cornwall. The quiet coves and sandy beaches of the south coast and the rugged cliffs of the north coast (is) within easy reach of the estate, as well as the many delightful inland villages of Cornwall.

↑ (LEAVE 4 CLEAR HERE)

The luxury/caravans for hire are luxurious indeed. Each caravan has a refrigerator, cooker, shower and flush toilet, heating and colour television.

West Winds Holiday Estate offers a large grassed area w hard standing for touring caravans, each pitch being ~~served~~ served w water & electric mains. The pitches are separated by shrubs and trees ~~to~~ to give privacy.

You can be assured of a warm welcome at West Winds Holiday Estate.

↑ ALL IN CAPS PLEASE

Shutter and Company Limited ← caps

Photographic Society

A meeting is to be held on Tues (date please - Tues of next week), in the Society's Rooms, Fanshaw Buildings, Blackshaw Mills, at 7.30 pm. [Will members tender apologies to the secretary if it is known that such members cannot attend.

This is the last meeting to be held in the Society's Rooms. In future all meetings w/ be held at the homes of members and a rota is being drawn up and will be pinned to the notice/board in Fanshaw Building. If any member objects to this (proceadure), please let me know asap.
↕ (leave 3 clear line-spaces)

(Agenda) ← spaced caps
1 Minutes of last month's meeting
2 Apologies
3 Treasurer's report — monthly accounts
                          membership fees
                          competition fees
4 Secretary's report — use of rooms
                          equipment (slide projector,
                          studio lighting and wall
                          mounting boards)

5 Competition report
6 Rules of the Society
7 Lecturers
8 Outings
9 Any other business
10 Date of next meeting

RONALD HARRISON
Secretary

Please insert today's date

The Lapwing ← *underline please*

headlong

Winter is coming to an end when a strange shape appears in the sky. With very well-rounded and broad wings, its flight is often wildly erratic with slow flapping wing beats and often daring plunges which all form a very spectacular and aerobatic display. It is a Lapwing. The haunting cry which accompanies this daring display is a loud nasal "peese-weet" or a long "pee-r-weet", sometimes with variations from which the Lapwing derives its alternative name, Pee-Wit.

(*) This large iridescent greenish-black and white bird is a member of the Plover family, distinguished by its long wispy head plumage and black breast contrasting with pure white underparts and cheeks.

↕ Please leave 8 clear line-spaces

Although so many pairs share the same nesting area, the chance of actually finding a nest is quite a rare occasion as the nest and eggs are well camouflaged and the parent birds is most skilful in misleading predators and humans.

scrapes

A courting male Lapwing makes holes in the ground, showing the female Lapwing places where a nest could be made. The female selects a nesting place and lines it with dried grass. Eggs are normally laid in late March/early May and are a greenish colour with black marks. The chicks, guarded by a parent, usually the female, leaves the nest within a few hours and can fly after about 5 weeks.

also

The Lapwing is a good friend of the farmer as it feeds on many harmful insects. It feeds on earthworms which are brought above ground to the surface by the Lapwing treading the earth.

During the breeding season, the Lapwing can be seen in large gregarious straggling flocks on farmland, moor and marshes in England, and Wales Scotland and more or less all over Europe.

Please type the paragraph marked (*) in double-line spacing.

TYPIST — Please type headings and paragraphs as the CONSTRUCTION heading & paragraph

spaced caps

COLLINGHAM CLASSIC

Technical Data ← Type as it is here

The following technical data applies to the 350A and 360A models of the Collingham C— caravan.

Please leave 6 clear line spaces

CONSTRUCTION ← Do not underline

Side walls and roof panels with an outer aluminium skin (25mm) & inner covered plywood skin (3mm). The flooring is a frame work covered w 7mm of plywood with an insulation of 33mm.

Chassis Independent bar suspension w double shock absorbers. Adjustable corner steadies & jockey wheel.

Electrics 12 volt installation w auxiliary from towing vehicle. A charger & battery box are provided. Mains electric w 2 13 amp plug sockets.

BRAKES Overrun brakes & parking break. Reversing facility.

Windows Double glazed in tinted acrylic. All windows are fully opening. 2 ventilation openings in roof (440mm x 440mm).

Interior Fireproof foam upholstery (115 mm). Zipped covers for easy removal (covers are washable). Furniture is made from natural veneer. Roller Venetian blinds are fitted at all windows. The flooring is covered w hard-wearing vinyl in a choice of colours. The kitchen is equipped w a stainless steel sink, 3-burner top & a refrigerator operated by gas, 12 volts or 240 volts. The toilet compartment is fitted with a pull-down wash basin, mirror cabinet & shower tray.

AVOCET BUILDING SOCIETY *caps*

A*n*nual Report of the Directors

TYPIST – please type the first paragraph in double-line spacing

This year has been an exceptional one in terms of competition for lending and investors' funds. Base rates started the year at 12½ *per cent.* The outlook for inflation improved and rates fell to 10% in late spring. Mortgage rates finally settled at 11%. Later on in the year, *however,* base rates rose to 11% and mortgage rates rose to 12¼%.

financially

Reserves   Reserves increased by £38 million to £237 million. We aim for a progressive incre*a*se in reserves which will ~~mean~~ ensure that we are one of the most secure building societies.

Please type all following headings and paragraphs like the Reserves para.

MORTGAGES

Total advances amounted to £1,526 million, an increase of 29% over the previous year. 56,825 new advances were made, of which 42% were to first-time buyers. We provided 26,268 further advances for ~~present~~ *existing* borrowers.

DIRECTORS

Mr F H Roundle and Mr K Maddock, who are both now 68 years of age, will not be seeking re-election. It is to be recorded that we are grateful to them for their wisdom and common sense over the years.

ASSETS

Assets increased by 14.4% to £6,143 million. Mortgage assets represent 81.2% of total assets.

STAFF

The new Chief Executive will be Mr L Wilson. Our former Chief Executive, Mr P R Bemrose, has retired due to ill health. The General Manager (Mortgages), Mr R Simpson, has *also* retired. This appointment is to be advertised in the near future.

DEPOSITS

During the yr, we introduced a 90 day notice a/c with a monthly income facility. This a/c proved very successful. Our retail investment receipts totalled £2,923 million.

PLEASE INSERT THIS PARAGRAPH AFTER THE 'RESERVES' PARAGRAPH

PLEASE TYPE THE 'BONUS' SECTION AFTER THE 'UNIT-LINKING' SECTION

UNICORN ASSURANCE SOCIETY LIMITED

(CHAIRMAN'S STATEMENT) *spaced caps*

↑ *Please leave 4 clear line-spaces here*

NEW BUSINESS ← *underline this and the next 2 headings please*

*   Results significantly ~~better~~ improved than those for industry as a whole.

*   Self-employed pensions/ *increased* due to competitive contracts.

*   Insured retirement benefits ~~pensions~~ have shown a marked increase.

BONUS

*   Rates of reversion*a*ry bonus increased to record levels at the end of the year.

*   Rates of terminal bonuses being paid (is) higher - exceptionally so in most cases - than those paid on similar policies in previous years.

Excellent
*   ~~Marvellous~~ bonus results show that our company policies are the very best. ^*P*Policyholders can continue to expect the best
(*All*) value. ⌐*P*

UNIT-LINKING

unit-linked
*   The company entered the/market with a large range of contracts designed to compete with the best on offer.

*   Premiums of £25 million in just less than a year brought in the biggest venture of its kind undertaken by our company.

Consultants
*   ~~Specialists~~ specialising in unit-linking were appointed to give expert (advise) to intermediaries.

↑ *Leave 2 clear line-spaces here please*

All enquiries should be addressed to U ——— A ——— S ———
L ——— , Foster House, 46 Chester Road, Manchester, M9 6PQ.

↑ *All in caps please*

It wd be helpful if you cd enclose a stamped addressed envelope with yr enquiry — this helps to speed up the reply to you, an important factor when you are considering taking out an insurance policy with our company.

49

BROKEN MELODY ← spaced caps

Broken Melody is a band from Scotland which formed ~~about~~ approx 2 years ago, and determination to succeed has helped the band to keep going. The band consists of 4 young men.

↕

Please leave space here for photograph — leave 8 clear line-spaces

Mark Cunningham is the lead singer. He is 22 years of age and has been entertaining since he was 12 when he was a singer in a local band. He comes from Clydebank. Mark now writes all the material for Broken Melody. ← caps

Thomas
~~Tommy~~ Mitchell, who plays keyboard, is 25 years of age. Thomas is the serious member of the band. He was born in Edinburgh but moved to Clydebank when he was 15 He has known Mark since he was 12. Thomas started a career but later decided to become a full-time member of BROKEN MELODY.

Neil McCloughlin is the bass player. Neil is the smallest member of the band, standing at a mere 5' 3". He also comes from Clydebank, but prefers Edinburgh. Neil is 24 years of age.

on a future designer

The bands first single was released last yr but only reached the lower half of the charts. The long-awaited second single has now been released. It is called 'Try to Forget'. The band are at present working on a debut album 'Refreshing' and this will be released shortly. BROKEN MELODY will be touring England, Wales and Scotland in the near future.

Graham McCallion is the drummer. Graham is the odd man out as he comes from Ireland. He met the other 3 members of the band whilst on holiday in Scotland. Graham is twenty-four years of age.

NOTICE IS HEREBY GIVEN that there will be a meeting of

Inset → the HILL AND VALLEY WALKING CLUB on Mon, (date

5 spaces → please – Mon of next week), at 24 Grasmore Ave,

SKIPTON, North Yorkshire, BD22 7BG.

↑ (Please leave 4 clear line-spaces)

A G E N D A

1 Minutes of / the last meeting

2 Apologies

3 Secretary's report including:

(a) new members of the club

(b) retiring members of the club

4 Treasurer's report

5 ~~buying~~ Purchase of new mini-bus

6 Walk Leaders' joint ~~report~~ report including:

(a) walksheets

(b) mid-week walks

(c) maps

(d) new walk leaders

✗8 Walks for next month

✗7 Weekend in the ~~Peak~~ Lake District

9 Date of next meeting

(Stephen Butler) – caps

Secretary

---------------- (Please type broken line across page) ----------

Please delete & complete as necy and return to

Stephen B _____ at the above address.

I shall/shall not be attending the meeting of the Hill and

Valley Walking Club on Mon, (date please). If you cannot

attend the meeting, please state whether you are in favour

of a weekend in the Lake District – YES/NO.

Signed ---------------- Date ----------------

51

MINUTES of a meeting of the (Hill and Valley Walking Club) on Monday, *(caps)* (date please - see Task 11).

DOUBLE LINE-SPACING

Present   Peter Bairstow (Chairman), Stephen Butler (Secretary),
           Jean Oates (Treasurer), Alberta and Quentin Bancroft,
           Dudley and Stephanie Beech, Jack Pitt and Elsie Greene

(leave 2 clear line-spaces here)

1   The minutes of the last meeting were read and approved.

2   Apologies were received from Jim Blade and Kevin Smith.

3   The (Secretarys) report was read and approved:

(a)   it was reported that 3 new members had joined the club - John
      and Mary Bradford and Lewis Jones;
(b)   it was reported that Ernest and Hilda Farrow had retired.

45 It was decided to purchase a new mini-bus and Dudley Beech
volunteered to gather information on prices etc and report back at
the next meeting.

(84 The Treasurer's report was read and approved.)

6   The Walk Leaders' joint report was [approved] [and] [read]:

(a)   it was proposed and seconded to have mid-week walks during the
      winter months;
(b)   walksheets have now been prepared for use by members;
(c)   new maps have been purchased covering North Yorkshire;
(d)   (see below) ✗

7   The Secretary is to draw up a list of *venues and* ~~hotels~~ hotels in the Lake District
and report to a special meeting of the club on *a date yet to be announced.*

8   The list of Sunday walks for *next month will be circulated to all members asap.*

Peter Bairstow ← *underline each line and*
Chairman   ← *leave one clear line between*

(d) It was ~~proper~~ proposed and seconded that Dudley and S — B — be appointed walk leaders.

9 The date for the next meeting was fixed for the third Mon of next month.

Please insert ✳ as 6(d)

TYPIST - please type the first paragraph in double line-spacing and the remainder in single line-spacing

"A garden is a lovesome thing, God wot!" - a line from a poem by T E Brown. A garden is indeed a lovesome thing. A garden is the haven to relax in, but it is also a valuable asset. A well-kept and well-designed garden adds considerable value to the house home. As yr garden matures, so does yr investment.

Please leave 6 clear line-spaces

Add interest to the garden w a patio and sun lounge - somewhere to sit and relax in the warmth of the sun - an extention to yr living room wh can be used through_out the yr. Paved areas are very easy to maintain and can be decorated w a variety of potted plants to give colour and fragrance. The installation of garden lights lets you enjoy yr plants in the evening as well as making yr house less attractive to burglars. ||If you look after a lawn all the yr round, it will keep attractive and pleasent to the eye. In the autumn, spike the lawn and give it a top dressing of fertiliser food and rake away unwanted moss. Watch out for worms - they are good for plants but not for grass. Regular mowing of yr lawn from early spring sun summer keeps it looking green and neat. Spring in the garden is a/ beautiful time. Daffodils, tulips, snowdrops and wallflowers all give that welcome touch of colour after the winter months. Spring is the time time to start preparing the beds for the bedding plants to be planted in late May. The long, lazy, hazy days of summer are days to be spent in the garden. Relax in the beauty of the glorious colours.

A garden is indeed a lovesome thing.

(Elterwater and little Langdale) — caps

A circular walk of about $7\frac{3}{4}$ miles

                    little
The walk starts from the ⌐car park approx 1 mile from
Skelwith Bridge on the Elterwater ~~road~~. Opposite the
car park entrance, there is a gap in the wall and
from here a path ~~leads~~ leads down to the river.
Follow the path to the right towards Elterwater
village. // In the village turn left over the bridge.
Walk on this road until it forks. Take the right-hand
fork and follow the unmetalled bridleway, climbing
(steaply.) At the kissing gate, turn left and walk
down to little Langdale.

On coming to a road, turn left & after approx $\frac{3}{4}$
mile a small farm is reached. Follow the sign⌐post
marked "Bridleway" to the distant wood. Follow the
left-hand path to the waterfall — Colwith Force.
From here follow any of the many footpaths down
thro' the wood until the road is reached. // Turn right
~~on the road~~ and walk on until you ~~see~~ a stile on the
left
~~right~~, go over the stile, across ~~a~~ the field and thro' a
wood. This soon opens out into a meadow. Follow
~~the~~ path to/a kissing gate.

⬆ (Leave 8 clear line-spaces for a map)

Go thro' the gate onto a narrow road and almost
opposite there (are) a stile w a path between 2
hedges. Follow this path to the farm⌐yard and
then keep to the right-hand path until the
main road is reached. ↩

Turn left to Skelwith Bridge and left again to
the slate/works.

Leaving the slate works, follow the path thro'
the woods, passing Skelwith Force, into the meadows.
Head
~~Head~~ for the ~~coppice~~ coppice in the middle of the
field and once here the (style) you started off
from can be seen on the right.

Left margin (vertical): Leave this village at the signpost to Stang End, via the footbridge over Greats Langdale Beck.

Section 3   Task 15 (approx 300 words)

(SAFETY AT WORK) ← *spaced caps*

Please type the "Look where you are going" section after the "Do the job properly" section

REMEMBER THESE IMPORTANT POINTS!

↕ *Please leave 2 clear line-spaces here*

Wearing the right clothing

1   In certain areas of the factory, there (is) signs to indicate that it is advisable ^to wear, in addition to overalls and caps, goggles, ear protectors and gloves.

2   Flat-heeled shoes in good condition should be worn. High-heeled ^or badly worn shoes are more ~~than~~ likely to cause you to fall.

3   Long hair can become trapped in machines with drastic results. Make sure that your hair is properly covered with a cap.

↕ (Just one clear line-space here)

Look where you are going

1   Be (carefull) when using doorways which are used by both vehicles and pedestrians.

2   Look both ways before stepping into gangways that are used by vehicles.

3   Each lift has a notice which indicates the maximum ^safe working capacity. Never overload lifts.

Do the job properly

1   Follow instructions and report defects on machines.

2̶3 Make sure that all guards are properly in position before operating a machine.

3̶4 Never tamper with safety interlocks. This equipment is provided for your safety.

2 A machine must be SWITCHED OFF when not in use at the main power supply. A machine must also be switched off when being ~~overhauled~~ cleaned.

PLEASE LEAVE 3 CLEAR LINE-SPACES

PLEASE TYPE ALL IN CAPS *Your co provides adequate resources to maintain good and safe working conditions but accidents still happen Many accidents could be prevented by a resp approach to safety matters. Each individual shd help in a positive way to reduce the risk of accidents.*

55

See Task 1 in this Section for addresses

BOWFALL DAMP & TIMBER CO LTD

Specialists in Remedial Treatment

spacedcaps

REPORT   (reference B.RD.29/54)   *← leave 3 clear line-spaces here*

Clients' Names   Mr and Mrs N McIntyre

Clients Address   23 W_____ A_____, SCARBOROUGH, North
                      Yorkshire, SC12 3HN

Site Address   61 M____ C_____, SCARBOROUGH, North
                      Yorkshire, SC18 ~~4PW~~ 4 PW

Description of Property   Semi-detached

Construction of Property   Stone/Pebbledash

Age of Property   Pre-war

Cavity of Property   8" - 12" wall

RISING DAMP Moisture meter readings were taken on *all* ground floor
walls where accesible at the time of inspection. In places the
original damp proof course was broken down.

A high moisture content was apparent in certain areas.

Ventilation   *sufficiently*

The property is ventilated.

Duration   *1½*

The work will take ~~2~~ days.

TYPIST - please type all headings and paragraphs like the RISING DAMP paragraph

Treatment Costs

£~~5~~ 675 plus VAT.

TREATMENT A damp proof course (chemical treatment) to be injected as stated in the Specification and any necy treatment to woodwork & plasterwork. Replastering to a finish coat.

PLEASE TYPE THIS PARAGRAPH AFTER THE VENTILATION PARAGRAPH

CAPS WITHOUT UNDERLINING

Silver Triangle Insurance Company Limited

Making a Claim

Section

The first thing to do is to check the appropriate policy/ to make
certain that what you are proposing to claim for is, in fact,
*i*nsured.

or telephone

DOUBLE LINE SPACING
Inform us as soon as possible by letter/ that you wish to make a
claim. We will then post off a claim form which you must complete
and return to us with any supporting evidence that we may ~~require~~
within 28 days of the incident.
need

few
For any other repairs or replacements, please obtain a*n*/ estimate*s* and
send (it) to us. We must have an opportunity to see any damage and
also approve an estimate before any work begins. You may be
informed, depending on the cost of the work involved and the
seriousness of the damage*s*, that you can go ahead and get the work
done before your claim is ~~finally~~ settled.

Check policy condition 9 on page 24 of your policy booklet for full
information relating to claims. If the claim is for damage to property and temporary repairs are ~~needed~~ to prevent further damage,
necy
you should make arrangements for them to be carried out ~~as soon as~~ *immed*
~~possible~~. Keep any bills for such work as they may be part of your
claim.

We will ALWAYS send a representative to see you if there
is serious damage. This may be either an independent loss
adjustor or one of our own inspectors. He/she will advise
you what to do immed and also let you know what
further info will be necy.

Finally, when all required information is available, we will agree
with you the amount payable.

⇕　(PLEASE LEAVE 5 CLEAR LINE-SPACES)

Please address any queries or claims to your insurance agent, John
Gelder (Insurance Consultants) Ltd, Holland House, 45 Central
~~Road~~, Leeds, West Yorkshire, LS1 2GA.
Ave

NB The new telephone number of your agent is Leeds 54789.

PLEASE TYPE THIS PARAGRAPH
ALL IN CAPITALS

SHUTTER AND COMPANY LIMITED

lower case, initial caps
and underline

PHOTOGRAPHIC SOCIETY

MINUTES of a meeting of the above Society held on Tuesday,   _see Task 5 for date ,_
in the Society's Rooms.   _leave 3 spaces_

PRESENT: Mr S Stevenson (Chairman)   Mr S Goddard
           Mr R Harrison (Secretary)   Ms B Wood
           Ms V Hanson (Treasurer)   Mrs C Whittick
           Mrs M Allen   Mr F Young

1   The minutes of the last meeting were approved and read.

2   Apologies were recieved from Ms A Court.

3   Treasurer's report   _leave 1 clear line-space_
    (a)   The monthly accounts were presented and approved.
    (b)   It was decided to increase the membership fees to £10 _per annum._
    (c)   It was ~~agreed~~ _decided_ that a fee of 5p per print or slide be
          introduced for entry into competitions.

4   Secretary's report   _1 clear line-space_   _out of Society's funds_
    (b)   It was agreed to purchase, subsidised by the Company, a new
          slide projector, studio lighting and wall mounting boards.
    (a)   The Society's Rooms are to be redecorated by the Company.

5   It was reported that entries in ~~the~~ competitions had increased.

6   The following rule was added to the Society's rules: "Society
    members are allowed to bring one person to meetings.".

7̷8   It was decided that the Chairman should seek new lecturers for the
    slide shows in the coming session.

8̷7   An outing was ~~decided~~ _arranged_ for the Society to visit the Parish Church
    on a date to be announced ~~at a~~ later. ~~date.~~

9   It was agreed that the next meeting of the Society would be held
    on the second Tuesday of next month at the home of Mr F Young.

    Please leave 2 clear line-spaces here

R ____   H ____

Sec   _see Task 5 in this Section_

58

SAVE YOUR MONEY *← spaced caps & underline*

MERCURY UNIT OVEN

This oven is a "little gem". It will transform your caravan or
holiday home. Set out below are all the details you need to know.

APPEARANCE   Attractive in style in a coal grey colour with red
(and check on) trim and control knobs. The smoked glass door enhances
the appearance and also allows the user to see cooking
without having to open the door.

CONTROLS The control knob is easy to use to operate the Mercury Unit
Oven. Clear red graphics show the position of the control knob - on,
off low, high and medium. The control knob is operated simply by
pushing and turning.

ACCESSORIES   The Mercury Unit Oven is supplied with 2 shelves and a *(free)*
bottom baking sheet. Also, as a gift if you order an oven from us, a
Yorkshire Pudding Baking Tray is supplied.

SAFETY   There is a device fitted to ensure that the supply of gas is
switched off automatically if the flame ~~goes out~~ expires.

SIZE   The Mercury Unit Oven is big enough for a 4 1/2 lb chicken or
a typical family Sunday roast. It has 3 shelf positions to enable
variable cooking. The overall width is 49 cm, the height is 46 cm
and the depth is 41 cm.

STOCKISTS   The majority of caravan accessories shops stock the
Mercury Unit Oven or you can order *one* by post, Visa welcome, from
Mercury Unit Ovens, 114-116 Mount View Lane Industrial Estate, LEEDS,
LS3 5DE. Order one today from us and save £13.60!

The corresponding opening sizes are 45cm , 41cm & 39 cm.

PRICE The recommended retail price of the M — U — O — is £169.50ᵖ⁹, but for a limited period we wl supply one for only £155-99.

PLEASE TYPE THESE HEADINGS & PARAGRAPHS IN THE SAME STYLE AS THE "APPEARANCE" PARAGRAPH

WEST WINDS HOLIDAY ESTATE

Conditions of Booking   ← _underline please_

↕ PLEASE LEAVE 5 CLEAR LINE-SPACES

1   All persons undertake /_not_ to do anything which, in the
opinion of the management of the estate, is detrimental to
the interests of others, or against the rules of the estate
which are displayed in the office/. _and in all hire_ ~~caravans~~
personal   caravans

2   The estate will not accept liability for any/injury,
loss /or damage which may be suffered by any person during
their stay at the estate.

3   A ₕirer of a caravan must be over 18 years of age.

4   Any child under ₆1̶0̶ years of age must be accompanied to the
washrooms, toilets and shop on the estate.

5   Deposits are not returnable unless the hirer is covered by
our Insurance Scheme*.

6   Hire _caravans_ must be left in a clean/ _and tidy_ condition and
any ⟨brakages⟩ or damage will be claimed from the hirer.

7   The management of the estate reserve the _right to enter any_ _hire_
caravan for the purposes of/repair. ⟨_mainienance or_⟩

8   The management of the estate reserve the right to refuse or
terminate
~~cancel~~ any booking application at their absolute
discretion.   , _if no deposit is recd,_
                                                          the reservation
9   Provisional bookings will be held for 8 days and/will be
cancelled ~~if no payment received~~.

* PLEASE ENQUIRE ABOUT THE INSURANCE SCHEME WHEN YOU MAKE A BOOKING.

IT ONLY COSTS £4 PER/WEEK.

10 _Dogs shd be exercised in the areas_
specified on the estate and shd be
kept on lead at all times.

60

☐ SECTION 4 — GENERAL

Section 4   Task 1 (approx 210 words)

(PLEASE TYPE FIRST PARAGRAPH IN DOUBLE LINESPACING)

(Tips on looking after your new camera) ← caps

Tough and durable though your new camera is,
it is a precision/optical instrument and careless
handling can cause irreparable damage.
Observe the following tips and your camera
should give many years of service.
↑↓ (Please leave at least 38mm (1½") for diagram)
Camera controls are designed to work with the
minimum of pressure. If you find you are using
① ~~undue~~ ~~unnecessary~~ force, you are doing
something wrong and may cause damage. [Keep
all lens, mirror and prism surfaces free from
dust and fingerprints. These surfaces should
not be cleaned with a dry cloth or tissue —
you will scratch the surfaces — use a
blower/brush.

When [removing] or [mounting] a lens, prevent
the entry of foreign matter and take care not
to damage the rear elements of the lens.

If condensation should form on the lens
due to extreme conditions (cold or high humidity), dry
the camera thoroughly at room temperature
and then store in a cool, dry place.

Always store your camera in the case and
if the camera is not to be in use for
several weeks, remove all batteries.

(PLEASE EMPHASISE THE ~~final~~ FINAL PARAGRAPH)

61

LAKE DISTRICT PHOTOGRAPHIC HOLIDAYS

Residential photographic courses in/ the Lake District's spectacular countryside. //Why not combine your holiday with your favourite ~~pastime~~ hobby?

In a series of autumn courses which are open to all photographers, (Fernside House) offers the (caps) following facilities –

PLEASE INSET THESE ITEMS BY 6 SPACES

* First-class tuition on (a) ~~one to one~~ individual basis
* Studio and dark room facilities
* Five Six acres of garden with hides
* lecture(s) – | landscapes, | general photography, portraits and printing techniques
* (Excellent standard of comfort)
* Accompanied walks with photographic viewpoints
* Delicious food
* Maximum number on any course – 10

⇕ (PLEASE LEAVE SPACE AT LEAST 38mm (1½"))

Please write or telephone for a brochure to

(Lake District Photographic Holidays) (caps)
Fernside House
Pooley Bridge
PENRITH   (Telephone 08536 4020)
Cumbria
CA10 3RS
←

62

(PLEASE KEEP ABBREVIATIONS)

FIRST PARAGRAPH IN DOUBLE LINE-SPACING PLEASE

ORDER NOW — (by post!) ← caps

The following is a ~~list~~ selection of items available from our special lines at reduced prices if ordered now. Hurry and fill in the application form and post today!

DUVET COVERS — single size, 135cm x 200cm. Various patterns, including "Sleeping Dogs". Matching pillow cases, 75 cm x 150 cm. Curtain

(also) material to match, 130cm.

LEAVE AT LEAST 76mm (3") ACROSS HERE FOR THE LENGTH OF THESE 4 ITEMS

MACS — ~~a~~ cape-type waterproofs in various lengths, 102 cm to 117 cm. Be seen in the rain in these bright colours — yellow, orange and green.

DESIGN YOURSELF T-SHIRT — plain white T-shirt with fabric pens to design your own pattern. T-shirts come in 6 sizes from ~~to~~ 70cm to 120 cm.

BITS-BAGS — cheer up your |kitchen| or |bedroom| with a gaily coloured bits-bag. Useful for shoes and socks or even notes and recipes. Various patterns including /dolls and teddybears.
clowns,

Use the ~~applic~~ application form at the back of your catalogue and post it to us without delay.

(PLEASE EMPHASISE, USING ANY TYPING METHOD, THE LAST PARAGRAPH.)

KEEP ANY ABBREVIATIONS

SPLASHES OF COLOUR IN YOUR GARDEN

↑ PLEASE LEAVE 3 CLEAR LINE SPACES

Colchicum

The Colchicum produces mauve or white flowers and is very similar to the crocus. Bulbs can be planted in any soil type but the soil must be well-drained. The bulbs should be planted about 10 cm down. The planting time is late summer.

Please leave space for photos across here at least 64mm (2½") for as long as the first 2 paras

Muscari

Muscari are usually blue in colour, although there is a pale purple variety. The flowers are formed of tiny bells. They will grow in any well-drained soil. The bulbs should be planted 5 cm down in late summer to early autumn.

The muscari grows between 20 and 23 cm.

Galanthus

Galanthus, commonly known as the snowdrop, is the beautiful pearl of the garden. The white, delicate hanging flowers usually appear just before spring and is a welcome sign in the garden. Most types of garden soil are suitable.

Photos to be here - leave space at least 102mm (4") for as long as these 2 paras

Narcissus very

This is a popular bulb, along with the daffodil, and varies in height from 20cm to 8cm. The bulbs are best grown in groups but the dwarf species are suitable in the rock garden. Bulbs should be planted in late summer to early autumn.

102 mm at least

PLEASE USE DOUBLE LINE SPACING FOR FIRST PARAGRAPH

TRAVEL COVER ABROAD — spaced caps

There have been many reports about the dangers of travelling abroad unless personal and medical insurance have been taken out and this can be quite a costly item. Rusco Insurance Limited offers to existing clients a comprehensive cover at a very reasonable cost price.

This cover replaces your normal Rusco benefits which are not applicable outside the United Kingdom. Set out below are details of our cover[1].

PLEASE INSET 6 SPACES

All medical expenses, including hospitalisation .... up to £80,000

Loss of belongings (luggage) .... up to £800

Cancellation of travel .... up to £450

Loss of money (cash) .... up to £200

Accident cover .... £5,000[2]

Overseas medical help (including homeward journey)

A separate document is available giving full (caps) details of conditions from Rusco Insurance Limited, Newbridge House, High Street, Skipton, North Yorkshire, BD23 5EL. Other leaflets are available giving information about our many different insurance covers.

PLEASE LEAVE AT LEAST 25mm (1") HERE

(1) Only available if you already hold insurance with the Company.

(2) For death or loss of limb.

PLEASE CHANGE Rusco to Rucso throughout

PLEASE CHANGE
bungalow
to
house

CHARLES RIDDIOUGH ESTATE AGENCY LIMITED
CHARTERED SURVEYORS AND AUCTIONEERS
↕ (leave space here of at least 25mm (1"))

Trimmingham Area

Detached stone-built (1864) bungalow for sale,
set in beautiful gardens, within easy
reach of HALIFAX, yet in a country
setting. The bungalow comprises:-

* ⟵⟶
# PLEASE
LEAVE SPACE
HERE ACROSS
(MARGIN TO
PARAS) OF AT
LEAST 38mm
(1½")

DOWNSTAIRS - hall (18' × 5'3") with oak
panelling; combined cloakroom/utility
room; lounge (23' × 16') with feature
stone fireplace and timbered
ceiling; dining room (16' × 15'3") with
attractive walnut fireplace; superb

(luxury
breakfast) kitchen, fitted with all modern
appliances but in keeping with
the character of the property.

OUTSIDE - stone-built double garage
with /useful loft; greenhouse and attract-
ively designed gazebo; various
out-buildings; the mature garden
is well-kept and offers seclusion.

* ⟵⟶

* ⟵⟶

(FIRST FLOOR - master bedroom with
⊘ dressing room en suite; 3 other.
further excellent double bedrooms;
bathroom with modern suite and
shower; separate wc.)

(RETAIN ALL ABBREVIATIONS)

66

Section 4 Task 7 (approx 190 words)

FIR TREES LEISURE CENTRE

Superbly

Come and visit our fantastic leisure centre, housed in a converted barn, fitted with pine walling throughout. [We are proud to offer the following facilities.

PLEASE USE DOUBLE LINE SPACING AND INSET AT LEAST 19mm (3/4")

Jacuzzi
Solarium
Indoor heated swimming pool
Trimnasium
Sauna
Squash courts
Basketball/netball courts
Health food restaurant

There are excellent changing facilities provided. The leisure centre is set in 6 acres of beautiful woodland with facilities for jogging, hockey and football.

outdoor

PLEASE LEAVE SPACE FOR PHOTO – AT LEAST 38mm (1½")

We are open from 9am to 9 pm. Children are welcome but must be accompanied by an adult if under 12 years of age.

Daily membership .... £1.00 per adult, 50p per child*

Weekly membership .... £5 per adult, £2.50 per child

Monthly membership .... £18 per adult, £9 per child

PLEASE EMPHASISE

If you wish to book any facility in advance, please telephone 0274 673455 any time between 10 am and 1 pm.

* Any child under the age of 12 years

MURRAY LIFE INSURANCE SOCIETY

PHEASE EMPHASISE
Murray Security Plan
WHEREVER IT OCCURS

A cheque on retirement

Now is the time to start planning your retirement, although this seems a/very long way off. If you would like enough money to spend your retirement how you choose, a Murray Security Plan can help.

PENSION
Whatever the state pension will be when you retire, look at today's figures and see how they compare with your weekly outgoings.

PLEASE
LEAVE SPACE
HERE AT LEAST
76mm (3") FOR AS
LONG AS THESE 3 ITEMS

RETIREMENT FUNDS

A Murray Security Plan can help you to boost your funds. For as little as 50p, you can (a day) look forward to receiving a substantial cash sum when you are 65. [This could be enough to make your dreams come true – a cottage in the country, a trip abra abroad, or help towards your family's future.

Investment ←(type as above 2 headings)

With a Murray Security Plan, you decide how much you want to invest – from £10 a month up to £45 or more. The sooner you start to save start an investment, the greater the returns will be.

⊘ Enrolment is simple easy. Decide how much you want to invest each month and get in touch with us as soon as possible. Nothing could be ae easier – either write to us or give us a ring – you have our address and telephone number.

(PLEASE CHANGE house to home)

Protection of Property   *(PLEASE TYPE THESE 2 HEADINGS IN CAPS)*
Guard your home against burglary

Doors

It is a good idea to always leave your house by the same door. Any other external door can then be secured from the inside. The door you leave from is then the only door you need to fit with a deadlock.

There are various types of deadlocks which are shown below.

(PLEASE LEAVE SPACE AT LEAST 38mm (1½"))

External doors which are not used for exit can be fitted with security bolts. Special attention should be given to patio doors. It is possible to fit a dead lock on some patio doors but there are locks designed specifically.

Windows

(PLEASE LEAVE SPACE HERE AT LEAST 64mm (2½") FOR AS LONG AS THIS PARAGRAPH)

All windows should be fitted with key operated locks (with removable keys). On some types of windows, it is better to lock the frame. The majority of new windows now can be locked in a ventilation position – ideal for bedrooms.

Remember to lock all windows and doors on leaving your house, even if it is only for a few minutes. It does not take a burglar long to get into your house. It is a good precaution to have a 'door viewer' fitted to enable you to see who is knocking on your door.

Keep you and your home safe and protect your family and possessions.

(Please emphasise the final sentence using any typing method.)

Please retain abbreviations

CHEESE STICKS ← Spaced caps

These sticks are/easy to make in a micro~wave
oven and if ~~brown~~ wholemeal flour is used,
the cheese sticks will have an attractive colour
and ~~a pet~~ appetising flavour.

↑ PLEASE LEAVE SPACE AT LEAST
↓ 25mm (1")

Preparation time – 5 minutes
Cooking time – 1½ minutes
Makes 12 sticks

PLEASE INSET 12 SPACES AND USE DOUBLE-LINE SPACING	100g (4 oz) wholemeal self-raising flour
	Pinch of dry mustard powder
	25g (1 oz) cheese, grated
	50g (2 oz) butter or margarine
	Salt and pepper
	Small amount of water

Sieve flour and mustard into a bowl. Cut the
butter into small pieces and add to bowl.
Rub in until mixture resembles bread~crumbs.
Add cheese and seasoning and stir together. Add
water to make a firm dough. Knead the dough
into a ball on a floured surface and roll out
to 6mm (1/4"). Cut into sticks approximately
51mm (2") long and 3mm (1/8") wide. Place half
the quantity in microwave and cook on HIGH
setting for 3/4 minute. Cook the remainder
in the same way. Leave to cool on a
baking rack.

TYPIST - PLEASE EMPHASISE THE FINAL SENTENCE

HELP TO CATCH A THIEF!

ALARMS AND SECURITY — spaced caps

Video Recorders and Computers etc

It is best advisable to mark video recorders, either # visibly or invisibly, with your house number and postcode. Marker pens can be purchased at most in many shops. [Marking goods can be a deterrent to thieves but it also helps the police to identify stolen goods. Make sure you ~~all~~ costly goods and remember to up-date your insurance year by year.

insure

Please leave space here of at least 89mm (3½") for some diagrams.

A record of serial numbers should be kept of all valuable equipment.

Alarms

An alarm can easily be fitted to/recorders or other costly equipment. Luminous digital displays also advertise the fact that you own some expensive equipment.

video

It is a good idea to position video recorders or microwaves out of sight to someone looking in ~~a~~ window.

at the

Precautions

If you are going on holiday, remember to cancel milk and papers. Ask your neighbour to keep an eye on your house and perhaps go in every evening to draw the curtains. You can buy electronic switches to turn your lights on and off.

Take these few sensible precautions and make life difficult for the thief!

PLEASE EMPHASISE
YOU
WHEREVER IT OCCURS

The Ambler Training Centre — caps

gained by
The advantages/of attending a course at The Ambler
Training Centre include the following:

51mm
PLEASE
LEAVE
SPACE
ACROSS
HERE AT
LEAST
51mm (2")

You determine the days and times of your
course

You progress at your own pace

You are given an individual course to suit
your needs

You will be trained to examination standards

pleasant
You will be able to work in (an) /office
environment using the latest equipment

51mm

If you decide to apply, ~~it is~~ an interview will be
arranged when it will be determined which of our
courses will suit you.

***

We offer Typewriting, Shorthand (Pitman and Teeline),
Book-keeping and Computer/Word Processing Courses. We
also offer Refresher Courses in those subjects. All our
tutors are highly trained and you will be given
one-to-one tuition. [If further details are required,
please write to us at the following address:

The Ambler Training Centre
Stonegate House
Derwent Road
HALIFAX
West Yorkshire
HX3 6PW

*** — where shown, please
leave vertical space of
at least 38mm (1½")

Two nights in Paris for only £55! ← caps

This price is ~~fully~~ /inclusive of :

Please
meet
by
10
spaces
{
Super-luxury coach transport
Return sailings
Bed and breakfast in a first-class hotel
↗Visit to Notre Dame and Eiffel Tower ↓
↗Tour of Paris
Courier service

DAY OF DEPARTURE (Saturday)

We depart at 6am to drive to Dover. Refreshments will
be served on the coach. We will sail at ~~midday~~ noon
to Calais. On arrival, we reboard the coach for the
(Paris) drive to our hotel. The courier will check you
into the hotel and you will then be free to relax.

DAY IN PARIS (Sunday)
After breakfast we will drive into the
centre of Paris seeing such sights as The
Arc de Triomphe and The Opera. On arrival
at Montmatre you will have free time
before driving back to the centre of Paris
for lunch and shopping. Later in ~~the day~~
afternoon we will visit Notre Dame and
Eiffel Tower.

PLEASE
LEAVE
SPACE
HERE
⟵⟶
AT LEAST
89mm (3½")
FOR AS LONG
AS THIS
PARAGRAPH

DAY OF RETURN (Monday)

In the morning we will visit a hyper-market and
then
/continue to Calais for the return journey to Dover.
We will arrive back at our /home destination late at
night after stopping en route for ~~a meal~~ light
refreshments.

73

PLEASE CHANGE
Don't to DON'T
each time it
occurs

ELECTRICAL EQUIPMENT   ] lower case with
SAFETY HINTS   ] initial caps and underline

(PLEASE LEAVE 4 CLEAR LINE-SPACES HERE)

Read the operating instructions before using
equipment. Ensure that electrical connections
are correctly made and always switch off and
withdraw the mains plug when changing
connections. Always consult an expert if
in doubt about the installation and operation
of equipment.

PLEASE
INSET
15
SPACES
AND
LEAVE
ONE
CLEAR
LINE-SPACE
BETWEEN
ITEMS

Don't remove fixed covers.
Don't leave any equipment switched
on if unattended unless such is
designed for unattended operation.
Don't obstruct the ventilation of
equipment.
Don't use makeshift stands.
Don't expose equipment to moisture.

Never allow anyone, especially children, to put
anything into holes or slots of equipment and
never take take chances with electrical
equipment of any kind.

It is always better to be safe than sorry.

(PLEASE EMPHASISE THE FINAL SENTENCE)

GREENO ← spaced caps & underline

THE TURF THAT IS ALWAYS GREEN!

Greeno is very adaptable as it is available in rolls and tiles of varying sizes. Greeno transforms patios, porches, pools and paths as well as the lawn areas of your garden. Never again will you have worn patches on your lawn.

The unique design of Greeno makes it very hard-wearing and colour fast. Unlike grass Greeno is not slippy even when wet. Greeno's many strong polyethylene tufts actually remove dirt from shoes, leaving the garden in the garden. The only upkeep needed to maintain the appearance of greenko is a simple hosing down now and again.

excellent

102 mm
PLEASE LEAVE
SPACE HERE OF
AT LEAST
102 mm (4")
FOR A
PHOTOGRAPH

102 mm

easily
Greeno can be cut to your specification whether large or small. Installation is very simple and Greeno will always stay in place because of the non-slip backing surface. Greeno is available in major do-it-yourself stores as well as from our reliable mail order service.

PLEASE LEAVE
SPACE FOR
DIAGRAM HERE
AT LEAST
64mm (2½")
FROM MARGIN TO
FINAL
PARAGRAPH

For further details, please contact us at Greeno, Cox Works, 13-17 Bramley Road, Warminster, Wiltshire, BA16 3PG, or telephone us at 0985 739470.

PLEASE EMPHASISE THIS
FINAL PARAGRAPH

ARTS AND ANTIQUES — spaced caps

SHELF ANTIQUE CENTRE

Our representative will be in your area next week and we would be pleased to hear from you if you have any items which might interest us.

It could be well worth your while getting in touch with us if you have anything unusual or old.

We will give high prices for the following items:

Antique Furniture

PLEASE LEAVE SPACE ACROSS HERE FROM MARGIN TO PARAS AT LEAST 64 mm (2½") FOR SOME SKETCHES FOR THE LENGTH OF THESE 4 PARAS

Chair sets, tables, bookcases, cabinets, hall stands and tallboys

Silver, Brass and China

Any silver items, brass candle sticks, fenders and pans, china figures, tea sets, tureens, toby jugs and plates

Clocks

Carriage, mantle, wall, grandmother and grandfather

Jewellery

Hatpins, rings, brooches, lockets, bracelets and pendants

64mm

We are also interested in old toys and musical instruments - dolls, dolls' houses, mechanical tin toys, flutes, piccolos, concertinas and old wind-up gramophones.

Please ring us now - 0274 7864 and ask for George Mills

all in caps please

HALIFAX PIECE HALL was originally built for the local industries as a market place and is a fine display of eighteenth-century buildings. The Piece Hall now contains many crafts shops, as well as an art gallery, ~~museum~~ MUSEUM, tourist information centre and restaurant. Entertainments are regularly held in the courtyard.

HAREWOOD HOUSE, designed in 17(9)5 has a beautiful interior. There are magnificent examples of sculptured ceilings and plasterwork, as well as paintings by English and Italian artists. There is a bird garden in the grounds with many exotic species, ~~and~~ including macaws and flamingos. An adventure playground is provided for young children.

> LEAVE SPACE FOR PHOTO AT LEAST 76mm (3") AT THIS SIDE OF THIS PARAGRAPH

Harry Ramsden's (caps) is the most famous fish and chip restaurant in the world. This restaurant, with chandeliers and fine decor, is well worth a visit for a meal.

> PHOTO HERE - SPACE OF AT LEAST 76mm (3") FROM MARGIN TO THIS PARAGRAPH

TEMPLE NEWSAM House is a magnificent Jacobean (Tudor) House standing in almost 1,000 acres of ground. The House has many paintings, as well as a fine selection of porcelain, silver and furniture.

> PLEASE TYPE THE FIRST AND THIRD PARAGRAPHS IN DOUBLE LINE-SPACING

ASHDOWN PRIVATE HOTEL

We offer you good service, fine food and comfort. All our menus are carefully selected from cordon bleu recipes. Our meals are delightfully served, freshly prepared and cooked according to your taste.

Ashdown, being in a corner position just off Main Street opposite a small public garden, offers an open aspect from all windows, most of which have mountain views.

PHOTO HERE - LEAVE SPACE OF AT LEAST 89mm (3'½") AND TYPE THIS PARA IN DOUBLE SPACING

A short stroll through the village brings you to the lake and boating jetties. There are shops, golf course, putting green and tennis courts nearby.

LEAVE SPACE HERE OF AT LEAST 51mm (2") ACROSS TO COVER THESE ITEMS

* Comfortable lounge
* Colour television
* Private facilities
* Tea/coffee making facilities
* Ample parking space

PLEASE USE DOUBLE LINE-SPACING

Breakfast is served between 8.30 am and 9.30am and dinner is served at 1900 hours. Morning tea is served on request.

(VACANT POST) ← spaced caps

HARDWARE SUPPORT TECHNICIAN — INFORMATION TECHNOLOGY

(keep this abbreviation)

There is a vacancy in the Network Control Centre for a Hardware S——— T———. The (NCC) is responsible for installing a wide range of terminals and networking equipment, including word processors and mini-computers. H——— S——— Technicians are also involved in the selection and testing of new types of equipment and in constructing, developing and experimenting with new hardware configurations.

DOUBLE LINE-SPACING PLEASE

Candidates should have at least one year's computer experience, preferably with some exposure to data communications or user support. Applicants should be able to communicate effectively and have an aptitude for problem solving.

The appointment involves some travel and applicants should have a clean driving licence. [This is a Grade 7 position with opportunities for progression.

⇧ (PLEASE LEAVE 4 CLEAR LINE-SPACES) ⇧

Applications to Mr J F Anderson, Personnel Manager, Rowanberry PLC, Manchester Road, Preston, Lancashire, PR1 2DG.

(PLEASE HIGHLIGHT THIS FINAL PARA)

PLEASE EMPHASISE
MAXI-PLAN WHEREVER
IT OCCURS IN THE TEXT

(MAXI-PLAN) - spaced caps

Credit Protection by Wingrove Mail Order

↑↓ PLEASE LEAVE 2 CLEAR LINE-SPACES ↑↓

If your income suddenly stops, how would you manage to pay your monthly account? We have the answer for you. [We have arranged Maxi-Plan which will protect monthly payments of customers for only a few pence a month. If, for example, your outstanding payment is £12.00, your monthly protection premium will be 61p.

Maxi-plan protects you if

PLEASE
LEAVE
SPACE
HERE
OF AT
LEAST
38 mm
(1½")
FROM
MARGIN
TO
PARAS

- neither you nor your wife/husband are in employment and either of you are hospitalised for more than 28 days, your payments will be made whilst you are in hospital;

- either you or your wife/husband are off work for more than 28 days due to sickness, your payments will be made until you return to work;

- either ~~your~~ you ~~off~~ or your wife/husband dies, your account will be paid off in full.

It is easy to join Maxi-Plan. You will be automatically enrolled from the date of your next ~~statement~~ statement. If you do not wish to use this scheme, please write to us within 21 days. ‖ Maxi-Plan gives you peace of mind — take up our offer of security.

80

SECTION 5 — TABLES

Section 5   Task 1 (approx 150 words)

PLEASE TYPE ALL THE
BLOCKS IN THE SAME STYLE
AS THE SECRETARIAL BLOCK.
PLEASE RE-ARRANGE THE TABLE-
'SECRETARIAL' FIRST, THEN
THE "GCSE" BLOCK AND FINALLY
THE "OTHER" BLOCK

KEEP ANY
ABBREVIATIONS

ENROLMENTS

Course	Date	Times	
		Morning	Afternoon *
PART ③ FULL-TIME OTHER			
Day	14 September	1100 - 1200	—
Evening	15 September	1000 - 1100	—
Day/Evening	16 September	—	1300 - 1500
① PART FULL-TIME SECRETARIAL			
Day	9 September	1000 - 1100	1400 - 1600
Evening	8 September	1000 - 1100	1300 - 1500
Day/Evening	11 September	1100 - 1200	1300 - 1600
PART ② FULL-TIME GCSE			
Day	15 September	—	1300 - 1400 / 5
Evening	16 September	1000 - 1100	—
Day/Evening	18 September	1000 - 1100	1400 - 1500

* Only at the Central Campus

PLEASE CHANGE "FULL-TIME" TO
"PART-TIME" throughout the table

81

Interview Questions — caps

Type of question	Purpose	Question [1]	
		Form	Illustration
PROBE	Show interest	Noises	Umm? Er? Oh!
	Seek information	Extension	How do you mean?
	EXPLORE Find in detail	Reflection	You feel that ...?
OPEN	Establish rapport	Contact	Mutually shared experiences. Put respondent at ease.
	EXPLORE Find background	General	Please tell me about ...
	EXPLORE Find attitude	Opinion	How do you feel felt about ...?
CLOSED [2]	Establish facts	Yes/No	Are you ...? Do you ...?

[1] Be clear about your question before asking it.

[2] Remember (not) to ask too many closed questions.

caps

Please change Find to Explore wherever it occurs

82

LOOK AFTER YOURSELF AND YOUR FAMILY

Hospital Benefit Scheme ←caps

Age[1]	Payments		Children[2]
	Regular Scheme	Extra Scheme	
Yourself INSURED			
17-39 18-40	£2.85	£4.85 [3]	Add £1.80
41-50	£5.25	£7.60	Add £1.90
51-60	£8.00	£11.55	Add £2.00
61-70	£10.35	£15.10	Add £2.10
INSURED			
Yourself and Spouse			
PLEASE MAKE SAME STYLE AS OTHERS [17-39 18-40	£10.05	£7.40	Add £1.90
41-50	£5.00	£14.65	Add £1.80
51-60	£15.95	£22.15	Add £2.00
61-70]	£20.00	£28.90	Add £2.10
INSURED			
Yourself, Spouse and Family (Special Scheme)			
17-39 18-40	£4.55	–	–
41-50	£7.05	–	–
51-60	£9.90	–	–
61-70	£12.35	–	–

[1] of the oldest person in the family

[2] to include all children in either Scheme

TYPIST – (1) Please change Yourself to Insured each time it occurs in the table.
(2) Please change 17-39 to 18-40 each time it occurs.

(Keep abbreviations)

(Oven Temperature Guide) ← spaced caps

ITEMS	TEMPERATURE		GAS MARK
	°F	°C *	
PASTRY AND DOUGH			
Shortcrust	325	170	3
Small white bread	425	220	7
Large cake	350	180	4
MEAT AND POULTRY			
Long roast	325	160 (7)	3
Short roast	(300)	220	7
Stuffed pork chicken	425)	165	2
SMALL ITEMS			
(type same as others)			
Meringue	(110	225)	¼
Cream Puffs	200	400	6
Deep-frozen individual meals	170	225 (3)	3

* Temperature control °C is for fan assisted ovens

(TYPIST - please type MEAT AND POULTRY BLOCK FIRST)

TYPIST - Please type in order indicated by circled numbers

PLEASE KEEP ABBREVIATIONS

BUSINESS STUDIES - COURSES

Course	Room [1]	Sept - April		May - July	
		Day	Time [2]	Day	Time [2]
OFFICE PRACTICE ③					
OP.2	21c	Mon	6 pm	Tues	6.30pm
SHORTHAND ⑤					
S.1	21b	Wed	6 pm	Mon	6 pm
S.3	21a	Mon	6 pm	Tues	6 pm
TYPEWRITING ①					
T.1	21b	Tues	6.30pm	Mon	6pm
T.2	21b	Mon	6 pm	Tues	6 pm
T.3	22at	Wed	6.30pm	Tues	6.30pm
WORD PROCESSING ②					
✓ WP.1	16 b	Thurs	6 pm	Thurs	6 pm
WP.2	17a	Wed	6.30pm	Wed	6.30pm
WP.3	18a	Thurs	6.30pm	Thurs	6 pm
SECRETARIAL DUTIES ④					
SD.2	26c	Tues	5.30pm	Tues	5.30pm

S.2   21a   Thurs   6.30pm   Mon   6pm

[1] Subject to alteration

[2] All classes are for 2 hours - the time given is the commencement time

Please type Breakfast block first, then lunch and then Dinner

(Nutritional Values *) – caps

FOOD	ENERGY CONTENT		PORTION (GRAMS)
	JOULES	CALORIES	
Lunch			
Soup	630	250	150
Meat	2500	200	600
Potatoes	1050	300	250
Vegetables	630	200	150
Fruit	210	90	540
Dinner			
Meat	200	2500	600
Cheese	90 100	420	90 100
Fish	90 100	920	220
Vegetables	200	630	300
Bread	90 100	150	150
BREAKFAST ← (Please make this heading the same as others)			
Meat Bread	90 100	150	300
Milk	500	1250	300
Marmalade	20	250	60
Egg	—	4$\overset{2}{\cancel{8}}$0	90 100
Butter	20	630	150
Muesli	150	630	150

2

3

①

* Based on 20 per cent protein, 31 per cent fat and 49 per cent carbohydrate

TYPIST (a) Please change 90 to 100 wherever it occurs
(b) Please type the PORTIONS (GRAMS) column as the _second_ column

HOW MUCH ARE YOU WORTH?

This table shows approximately how much you will receive
at 65 years of age and how much your family would receive
if you died before 65. These figures apply to men. Details
are available for women.

Age	Monthly Investment	Returns	
		Life Cover [1]	Cash Sum [2]
	£	£	£
25-30 21-25 ⎫	15	58,876	6,226
31-35 ⎬		34,577	5,098
36-40 ⎬		19,980	4,082
41-45 ⎭		11,580	3,201
25-30 21-25 ⎫	50	122,935	13,000
31-35 ⎬		72,200	10,645
36-40 ⎬		41,718	8,523
41-45 ⎭		28,1834	6,685
25-30 21-25 ⎫	30	208,393	22,037
31-35 ⎬		122,390	18,045
36-40 ⎬		70,714	14,447
41-45 ⎭		47,9940	11,332

[1] This will increase due to bonuses.

[2] These figures are based on an investment return
of $10\frac{3}{4}$% per annum.

NB Further details are available for increased monthly
investments and of returns for persons over the age of
45.

PLEASE CHANGE 21-25 to 25-30 EACH TIME IT OCCURS

(Expandadoor) - caps please

Width of aperture ~~opening~~ for single doors		No of Sets required		Width of foldback	
		Set 2	Set 1		
	mm				mm
2' 6"	760	-	1	6½"	165
2' 10"	888	1	1	6 7/8"	175
3' 6"	1070	3	1	7 5/8"	195
3' 2"	965	2	1	7 ¼"	185
3' 10"	1170	4	1	8"	205
4' 2"	1270	5	1	8 3/8"	215
4' 6"	1475	6	1	8 ¾"	230
4' 10"	1370	7	1	9 1/8"	220
5' 2"	1575	8	1	9½"	240

✓ NB   If ~~a pair~~ two of doors is needed, check the measurement of half your aperture and order double the quantity of Set 1 and Set 2.

(5' 6"   1675   1   9   9 7/8"   250)

Please insert as the last item in the table

TYPIST   (1) Retain abbreviations
(2) Type the figures in the table in double line-spacing
(3) Please transpose the whole of columns Set 2 and Set 1 so that Set 1 comes first

Smithson DIY Central Heating System

(See How Much You Can Save!) ← caps

PROPERTY	COST *		SAVING
	FITTED	DIY	
③ DETACHED			
~~bedroomed~~ 3-roomed	£1840	£935	£905
~~bedroomed~~ 4-roomed	£2180	£1150	£1930
① TERRACE			
~~bedroomed~~ 3-roomed without attic	£600	£1225	£625
~~bedroomed~~ 3-roomed with attic	£715	£1405	£690
② ~~Semi~~ Semi-detached ← (make same style as other headings)			
~~bedroomed~~ 3-roomed	£1485	£725	£780
~~bedroomed~~ 4-roomed	£1640	£860	£760

* Cost will vary slightly dependent on type of system installed.

TYPIST - please change -roomed to -bedroomed throughout
  - please type in order indicated by circled numbers
  - please retain abbreviations

Please type Mallard section first, then Teal and finally Shoveler

POINTS OF IDENTIFICATION OF /SOME/ SURFACE-FEEDING DUCKS

Species	Differences	
	Male	Female
TEAL *(lower case, initial cap & underline)* (Anas crecca)		
Smallest European duck, very rapid flight in small flocks	Dark head, white stripe above wing, green eye patch	Speckled brown, green speculum
Mallard (Anas platyrhynchos)		
Rapid flight with shallow wing beats, orange legs	Green head, white ring round neck, brownish breast	Orange on bill, white tip on tail
Shoveler (Anas clypeata)		
Huge spatular-shaped bill, sits low on water	Green glossy head, dark chestnut sides	Brownish with blue shoulders

Please add the following as a ~~final~~ column headed Habitat

Opposite Mallard info	Any water, nests beneath undergrowth
" Teal "	Reedy streams, breeds on moors and marshes
" Shoveler "	Marshes and ponds, breeds on meadows and marshes

Films – Black and White
Guide for Photographers ◄──── caps

Film		Available	Uses	Grain *
Type	S≠peed			
Slow	12-50	Sheet/roll	(m-f) ◄─ △	(General, big enlargements)
Medium	50-200	Sheet/roll	General and studio	m-f
Fast	200-800	Sheet/roll	Artificial light, news reporting	m
Copying	8 - 20	Sheet/roll	Copying drawings etc	f
Infra red	4 - 100	Sheet/roll/ plate	Special effects	m-f
Reversal	32-100	Roll	Slide film	m
Lith	8-40	Sheet/roll	Line negatives	f

* m = medium, f = fine

Very fast   800-1600   Roll   Poor light   m

Typist – please type the "Uses" column as the final column of the table

Keep abbreviations

Please keep all abbreviations

TRAVELLING WITH CHILDREN ON OUR CRUISES

Percentage off Adult Fares* ← caps

Type of cabin	6 mths – 5 yrs Cruises		6yrs – 11 yrs Cruises		12yrs – 19yrs Cruises	
	602 604 605 606	608 611 612	602 604 605 606	608 611 612	602 604 605 606	608 611 612
	%	%	%	%	%	%
Family cabin **	75	70	65	60	55	50
4 berth, washbasin only	70	60	60	50	30	40
3 berth, all facilities	65	45	55	45	35	25
2 bedded, all facilities	25	20	20	15	20	10

* Babies under 6 months of age cannot be carried on cruises

** 2 bedded, with shower and wc, and 2 foldown upper berths

Typist – please type the Family cabin item as the last item in the table

92

Please retain abbreviations but do not use dittomarks

PART-TIME LECTURER – (Miss S A Stewart) – caps

TIME TABLE OF CLASSES

Class	Day	Period of Employment		Time of Class
		From	To	
Office Practice				
OP/1a	Mon	September	December	1000 – 1200 hrs
OP/1c	Wed	September	"	1400 – 1600 hrs
OP/2d	~~Thurs~~ Fri	"	June	1000 – 1200 hrs
Typewriting				
TP/1a	Mon	September	February	1800 – 2000 hrs
TP/1b	Wed	"	December	1830 – 2030 hrs
TP/2a	Tues	"	June	1000 – 1230 hrs
Word Processing				
WP/1a	Mon	March	June	1800 – 2000 hrs
WP/1c	Wed	January	"	1830 – 2030 hrs
WP/2a	Tues	September	"	1800 – 2000 hrs

Please make style of this block the same as the other two

TYPIST – please type the blocks in the following order –
Typewriting
Word Processing
Office Practice

Please change "memo" to "letter" wherever it occurs

LIAISING WITH PERSONNEL

Job Title	Department	Contact	
		Frequency ~~How often~~	Type
Manager	Production	Daily	Personal/telephone
Supervisor	Maintenance	Daily – several times	Personal
Chief Engineer	Maintenance	~~Daily~~ Weekly	Personal/memo
Engineer	Research	Monthly	Personal/~~Memo~~/telephone
Supervisor	Installations	Monthly	Telephone/memo ~~Personal~~/~~telephone~~
Accountant	Accounts	Monthly	Personal/telephone
Outside Supplies	Representative	Weekly	Telephone/memo

Engineer   Maintenance   Weekly   Personal/memo/telephone

TYPIST – please type the Department column in first column position (ie transpose the first two columns

Please change SO to SC each time

Ready-cut carpets in room size pieces

PLEASE TYPE ALL IN CAPS

These carpets are easy to trim to/your exact room measurements. All carpets have cushion foam backing and are available in brown, ~~to~~ blue and rose.

Number	Size	Price £	Instalments	
			20 weeks £	36 weeks £
POLYPROPYLENE				
CD/211	3m × 4m	41.60	2.28	1.32
CD 212	4m × 4m	54.50	2.99	1.74
PG 260	4m × 5m	66.00	3.63	2.10
PG 261	4m × 6m	72.80	↗4.62↗	↗2.68↗
PG 26̸2	4m × 7m	84.00	↘4.00↙	↘2.32↙
NYLON				
BM 103	³4m × 4m	43.80	2.³89	—
BM 104	4m × 4m	↗68.60↗	3.08	1.71
SO 203	4m × 5m	↘56.00↙	3.77	2.19
SO 206	4m × 7m	90.30	4.96	2.88

SO 204   4m × 6m   80.00   4.40   2.55

Typist- please type the NYLON block first

PLEASE LEAVE
2 SPACES AFTER
THE BRACKETS
CONSISTENTLY

REACTIONS BETWEEN SOME METALS AND OXYGEN

Symbol	Metal	Reactions	
		In heated air	In cold air
Na	Sodium	Forms oxide with burning	Forms a film of metal oxide
Al	Aluminium		
K	Potassium		
Ca	Calcium		
Fe	Iron		
Zn	Zinc		
↕ Leave 3 clear line spaces			
Cu	Copper	Forms oxide without burning	
Sn	Tin		
Pb	Lead		
↕ Leave 3 clear line spaces			
Au	Platinum	No reaction	No reaction
Pt	Gold		

Typist - please type the Metal column first

96

Please change "Private Hotel" to "Guest House" each time

HOLIDAY TIME *lower case, initial caps & underline*

1 night extra

Hotel	Price *		1 night extra
	2 nights	7 nights	
	£	£	£
CLASS 1 HOLIDAY			
Smith Hotel	75	207	10
Highfield Manor	65	189	10
Claremount Hotel	42	110	8
CLASS 2 HOLIDAY			
Ferndean Private Hotel	37	89	30
Restawhile	38	87	25
Atlantic View	35	80	14
CLASS 3 HOLIDAY			
Oak Wood Private Hotel	35	82	10
Park Private Hotel	32	78	89
Wood-lands Private Hotel	33	80	9

PLEASE MAKE SAME AS OTHER BLOCKS

* Per adult. The price includes bed, breakfast
and evening meal. The rates for children (12
years of age and under) are 40% of the adult
price on Class 1 Holidays, 50% on Class 2 Holidays
and 60% on Class 3 Holidays.

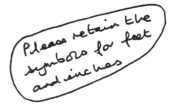
Please retain the symbols for feet and inches

New houses on the Larkspur Building Site Estate —caps

Type of Property	Measurements (1)		Price (2)
	House	Bungalows	
3-BEDROOMED SEMI-DETACHED			£34,000 – £38,250
Lounge	15' × 15'	16' × 16'	
Dining Room	14' × 12' 6"	15' × 14' 6"	
Kitchen	12' × 12'	12' × 12'	
Bedrooms 1 and 2	15' × 15'	16' × 16'	
Bedroom 3	10' × 9' 6"	11' × 6' 6"	
3 BEDROOMED DETACHED			£39,000 – £45,550
Lounge	17' × 16'	17' × 17'	
Kitchen	12' × 11' 6"	13' × 12' 6"	
Bedrooms 1 and 2	16' × 16'	16' × 16'	
Bedroom 2	15' × 15'	16' × 16'	
Bedroom 3	14' × 12'	10' × 12'	
4-BEDROOMED Detached caps			£48,950,000 – £57,850
Lounge	17' × 17'	17' × 16'	
Dining & Kitchen	15' × 12'	16' × 12' 3	
Bedroom 1	15' × 15'	15' × 15'	
Bedroom 2	14' × 12'	15' × 12'	
Bedrooms 3 and 4	12'6" × 10'	11'6" × 10'	

Dining Room 15' × 14' 16' 6" × 15'

(1) Bathrooms vary slightly but are all fully-fitted with a 3-piece suite.

(2) The prices vary between the figures given according to fittings required by the purchaser.

98

Retain abbreviations

SUNSPOT GARDEN FURNITURE

Add charm to your patio

Description	Price		Code*
	Kit Form	Assembled	
	£	£	
KEATS - traditional style with moulded arms, very durable for ~~out~~ outdoor use			
Chair	95	108	717
4 ft Seat	110.90	125	715
5 ft Seat	135	148	716
TENNYSON - a practical round table and matching chairs, ideal for the patio			
Round Table	2~~4~~50	-	809
Dining Chair	98	103	808
MILTON - simple yet classic style, ideal for a small garden			
3 ft Seat	92	102	610
5 ft Seat	130	115	611
Chair	85.50	95.50	612

→ make same as other blocks

* Add "A" to the Code if ordering assembled furniture.

TYPIST - please type the Price columns at the right-hand side of the table
- please type in this order, MILTON, KEATS, TENNYSON

(Keep all abbreviations)

(Please change 2500 to 2400 throughout the Task)

Garden Buildings

Type *	Size		Price inclusive of delivery
	Imperial (ft)	Metric (mm)	
APEX			
with 2 windows	7 × 5	2100 × 1500	£210.95
	8 × 6	2500 × 1800	£252.00
	10 × 6	3000 × 1800	£302.95
with 3 windows	8 × 6	2500 × 1800	£305.95
	10 × 6	3000 × 1800	£255.50
PENT			
with 1 window	7 × 5	2100 × 1500	£150.95
	8 10 × 6	2500 × 1800	£154.95
with 2 windows	8 × 6	2500 × 1800	£159.00
	10 × 6	3000 × 1800	£165.00
CHALET			
with a front height of 7ft (2100mm) and a rear height of 6ft (1800 mm)	7 × 6	2100 × 1800	£339.95

* All kits come complete with glass.

We have a superb range of garden buildings for DIY enthusiasts. All fixings are included and all you need is a screw driver, hammer and a knife. Come and see our range of DIY garden buildings. Our friendly staff will be available to give assistance in ~~this~~ choosing the right building for your garden.

100

☐ SECTION 6 — FORMS

Section 6   Task 1 (approx 30 words)

Will you please fill in the form headed AMBLER COACH SERVICES on behalf of Mr John Pickles.

Mr Pickles, his wife Patricia, and 2 children, Tracy, aged 7 and Thomas, aged 5, have decided to go on holiday. They are to go to stay at Sea Vista, Torquay, on Tour 22. They wish to leave Bradford on 23 May this year. Mr Pickles and family live at 27 Hillside Avenue, BRADFORD, BD16 2AF.

It has been decided to take out Holiday Insurance and therefore the amounts being sent are £20.00 (deposit) and £5.00 (Insurance). The Pickles' phone number is 0274 59657.

Mrs Pickles suffers from bronchitis, so "No Smoking" seats are required.

Will you please complete the form for me. I am applying for the post of Personal Secretary at John Paisley Ltd. My full name is Susan Jacqueline Williamson (Miss). I am single at the moment but hope to get married later this year. My home telephone number is 0827 88124. The following persons have given me permission to use their names as referees —

Mr D Benn, 3 Coutts Road, Bungay, Suffolk, NR34 6PE

Miss V Lake, 22 Park Road, Tenby, Dyfed, SA 54 2DW

I was born on 28 January 1969 and live at 16 Sefton Avenue, TAMWORTH, Staffordshire, B68 4PW.

Will you please type the following in the appropriate box.

French and German and I am at present on an Italian course

Date the form and leave it on my desk so that I can sign it before posting.

Thank you

Please fill in the Order Form on behalf of
Mr Andrew Stains of 22 Windermere Way,
MORECAMBE, Lancashire, LA2 8RT.
Mr Stains will pay by cheque.
The following items are required:

No	Description	Code	Price each	Total value
1	PA button	262	5.35	5.35
1	Cable coil	281	13.30	13.30
1	External bell box with sounder/strobe	234	33.95	33.95
x2	Internal PIR	2542	36.75	73.50
4	Door contact	254	1.05	4.20
1	Control box (keypad)	240	49.50	49.50

Total price £179.80

All the items are to be delivered to
14 Pine View Avenue, MORECAMBE, Lancashire
LA6 9SW

TYPIST — Please type the items in
ascending order of Code, ie 234 first.
There is not a lot of space to type
this list so please type the items
in single line-spacing.

PLEASE COMPLETE THE FLEXICARD LOAN APPLICATION
FORM.

Mr Prince is applying for a loan of £2,500
to help him buy a ~~new car~~ new car. Mr
Prince's christian names are John Frederick.
He lives at 49 Coniston Grove, (Shipley,) ⌐caps
West Yorkshire
ᴵ BD16 8RG. He was born on 22 May 1964.
Phone number (STD) 0274 59614. Mr Prince is
married and is living in his own home. He
works for Malvern and Company. He uses
the Strand Bank Ltd where his account
number is 0503 673456/2 at the Shipley
branch.

Mr Prince has a monthly salary of £929.67
(after deductions) and he pays out £340
per month.

Miss Rachel Sharon Simpson of Halifax is applying for a Savings Plan of £25 per month. Her birthday is on 9 March and she was born in 1965. Rachel is a Schoolteacher. She is not married.

Rachel has never suffered ill-health although she was in hospital last month. She doesn't take part in any risky activities and has never had an Aids blood test.

Reason for answering yes to the second question -

In hospital for two days with a broken leg caused by a fall down a staircase

Please complete the Job Sheet with the following details. Job No is SP/273
The work is being carried out for Mr Seamus Bairstow at 72 Mimbleton Road, DAWLISH, Devon, EX3 2PD

The job is
    New door to be painted and
    fitted with new handles

Action
1 Sand and prime
2 Sand and undercoat
3 Sand and final finish
4 Fix handles

Materials
Sandpaper   £1.20
Primer paint - grey   £2.55
Gloss paint - white   £2.95
Undercoat paint - white   £2.55
Door handles - grey   £7.49
                                 £16.74

The job should take 3 days and the employee to do the work is Stephen Pollard. His works number is 07

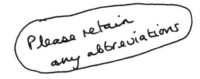

Please retain any abbreviations

This order is to be delivered to
J H Williams & Co Ltd, Unit 7, St John's
Trading Estate, RICHMOND, North Yorkshire,
DL3 2YT.

	Description	No	Code	Price each
④	Drum of Gortex oil (25 litres)	1	P68	£8.00
②	Roller bearing (30 x 10 x 5)	2	R445	£17.50
①	Seal kits for pneumatic cylinders (R1-50-25)	2	C662	£1-50
③	Oil seal (55 x 25 + 3)	1	P54	£3-75

The goods have to be delivered to the
Maintenance Department to a
Mr D H Johns who is expecting them
on Friday next.

The Order No is 03629 and the reference
is VM/FA. Please date the form with
tomorrow's date, as it is too late to go
out today.

TYPIST - Please also type the items
in the order indicated by circled
numbers

107

Mr and Mrs S Stephenson are having some new double-glazing work done. Please complete the Contract.
Mr and Mrs Stephenson live at 87 Cleveland Rise, Corston, BATH, Avon, BA8 6JN. The Stephensons request the following :-

Work may be done on any days apart from Mondays and Tuesdays

The following ~~items~~ windows have been ordered :-

		Width	Height
White/Clear	in the Dining Room	1100	1000
White/Clear	in the Kitchen	950	750
White/Clear	in the Rear Bedroom	1100	1550
White/Leaf	in the Bathroom	850	1300
Derby/Flemish	Rear Door	950	2150

The total cost is £1734.18

Cash price	£1507.99
VAT	£226.19
Total price	£1734.18
Deposit	£200
Balance	£1534.18

Delivery   Six to Eight weeks

Mrs Anne Hyde-Smith is applying for Propet to insure her dog, a poodle, against veterinary bills. Mrs Hyde-Smith lives at 8 Rosemount Way, CHELTENHAM, Gloucestershire, GL43 3TL

She requires the Platinum cover for Precious (her poodle) and will pay the annual premium of £53.00 by Access. Her credit card number is 0492 673 54261.

Mrs Hyde-Smiths telephone number is 0242 985671.

Precious is a female dog and is only 9 months old. She has only been to the vet once, for vaccination against distemper/hardpad, virus hepatitis and leptospirosis when she was 3 months old

Mr Holmes is requiring details of car insurance. His full name is Alan Rodney Holmes and he lives at 22 Fieldgate Avenue, SALTBURN-BY-THE-SEA, Cleveland, TS9 6EG.

Alan was born on 25 November 1962 and he works for Baywell Engineering Ltd as a Works Manager. He has been driving for 9 years and has a 60% No Claims Discount.

At present he owns a Renault 21, the GTS model which is a saloon. It has a 1700 cc engine, the year of manufacture is 1986. Registration number is D330 TCP and its value is £5,800. Alan requires Comprehensive cover. No-one else at all will drive the car apart from his wife who is 26 years old. Alan has never been convicted of a driving offence.

The cardholder completing this Booking Form is Peter Holmes. Will you please type in the details.

Peter and his wife, Jacqueline, are going to Puerto De La Cruz, Tenerife for 7 nights. They are to depart from Manchester on the 24th November this year and will fly to Reina Sofia. The holiday is costing £1590 and Peter's Visa card number is 0321687458 (5 6) 2310

Peter and Jacqueline will share a double room. Their son and daughter and friend are also going. Rachel, the daughter, will share a twin-bedded room with Sharon and their son, James, will have a single room.

The names should be shown as -

Peter	Holmes	HB	D
Jacqueline	Holmes	HB	D
Rachel	H ——	HB	TW
James	H ——	HB	S
Sharon	Stephens	HB	TW

Villa is the name of the hotel in Puerto De La Cruz. Insurance is required.

Peter's address is 22 Park Road, Oakes, HUDDERSFIELD, HD14 9SM

Keep all abbreviations

Jane Moore's form teacher, Mrs Haskew, has designed a form for completion by all pupils in the fourth year at St Peter's RC High School. An example for students is to be circulated. Will you fill in the form for Jane Moore of form 4B

Examing boards given in brackets. Don't type the brackets.

		Paper
(NEA)	English Language	—
(NEA)	English Literature	—
(NEA)	Mathematics	P & Q
(NEA)	German	Basic & Higher
(SEG)	Religious Studies	—
(LEAG)	Chemistry	1 & 2
(MEG)	History	—
(LEAG)	Biology	P & Q
(RSA)	Typewriting	1

Jane's Careers Officer is
   Mr Royston Blackmore

Jane lives at 26 Claife Road, WINDERMERE, Cumbria, LA8 6PQ

Keep all abbreviations

Please complete the delivery note with the following details.

Deliver after 2pm to Mrs. G. Macmillan of 23 Sycamore Grove, SHERBORNE, Dorset, DT9 6PE. Invoice to Cash Account, Top-plus Supplies.

⑤ CT64198R	Lift-off tapes	(Ref 62958)	10
② RB63156B	Nylon ribbon	(" 04058)	5
① RB62155B	Carbon ribbon	(" 03062)	10
③ RB74261B	Printer ribbon	(" 05215)	10
④ PP42065C	White bond (A4 size)	(" 04871)	500

The van route used is B and the number is 639

Please type the list of products in the order indicated by the circled numbers

113

Miss Elizabeth Milner is ordering a selection
of clothes for herself and her sister, Jane,
from Rags Fashions. Please type the order
form.

Code	Des.	Size	Quant.	Price	Subtotal
D23	Blue/white dress	~~10~~ 12	1	19.99	19.99
B46	White blouse	12	2	14.99	29.98
S19	Black skirt	10	1	16.59	16.59
T64	Blue t-shirt	10	2	9.6~~5~~	19.30
J12	Denim jeans	10	1	26.30	26.30
T66	Yellow t-shirt	10	2	9.65	19.30

Total   131.46

Miss Milner lives at Highbeck Farm, Pasture
Lane, SETTLE, North Yorkshire, BD24 3GT.
She is paying by cheque.

114

Alan Wright and his son, Lee Paul, aged 9 years, are entering a photographic competition. Please type in the necessary details.

Alan is entering 2 monochrome prints in the Animal category, 3 colour slides in the Plant category and 3 colour prints for Habitat.

Lee Paul is entering 3 colour prints in the Animal category, 1 colour slide in the Plant and 2 colour slides in Habitat.

Lee Paul lives with his mum and dad at 14 Goodway Gardens, WIDNES, Cheshire, WA4 7AP. The home phone number is 051-424 6744

There is no need to repeat the address and phone number in the CHILD SECTION — As above in both places will do.

8 at £1 = £8.00
6 at 50p = £3.00
£11.00

£11 enclosed

Eg					
Category	No	Slide	Print	Colour	Monochrome
Animal	2		X		X

BLANK FORMS FOR USE WITH SECTION 6

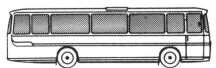

AMBLER COACH SERVICES

48 BRADFORD ROAD, HALIFAX
WEST YORKSHIRE, HX3 2NW

BOOKING FORM

Tour	Hotel	Depart Date

Number of Passengers .... adults .... children under 14

Please state seats required   Smoking/No smoking *

Name and address of person to whom correspondence should be sent

Name ....

Address ....

....

....

Tel No ....

Holiday Insurance required   YES/NO *

I enclose deposit of £

I enclose Insurance of £

Signature .... Date ....
*Please delete as required

© Macmillan Education (Mary Ambler, *Skills Success at Level 2*)

JOHN PAISLEY LTD

APPLICATION FOR THE
POSITION OF ....

Mr/Mrs/Miss*   Surname ....

First Names ....

Address ....

....

....

Postcode ....

Tel No (Home/Business*) ....

Date of Birth ....

Marital Status ....

Do you speak or read a foreign language?   Yes/No*
(If Yes, give details)

In the box below please give the names and addresses of two referees.

Signature ....

Date ....

Please delete as applicable

TRUMPET SECURITY SYSTEMS

66 Belle Vue Road, Preston, Lancs, PR2 8GT
Telephone 0772 870471

ORDER FORM

Code	Description	No	Price each	Total value
			£	£
Collected/Delivered *Please delete as applicable*			Total price	£

NAME ....

ADDRESS ....

....

....

Payment by Visa ☐ Cheque ☐ Cash ☐

Please insert X in box

If delivery address
different from above
please state

.... (Date)

FLEXICARD LOAN

APPLICATION FORM
Please complete all sections

Mr/Mrs/Miss/Ms*

Surname _____

First Name(s) _____

Address _____

_____

_____

Tel No _____ STD Code _____

Date of Birth   /   /

Single/Married/Widowed *   Home Owner/Tenant/Other *
Employee/Retired/Other *

Bank Name _____

Branch _____

Account No _____

LOAN REQUIRED FOR

LOAN REQUIRED — £

MONTHLY INCOME   £

MONTHLY OUTGOINGS   £

I declare that the information above is correct.

Signature .... Date ....

*Please delete as necessary

Endowment Savings Plan

APPLICATION FORM

Please indicate the monthly amount you wish to save and answer all questions.

* Please delete as appropriate.

Surname (Mr/Mrs/Miss*) ....

Forename(s) ....

Single/Married/Widowed*   Date of Birth   /   /

Occupation ....

YOU CAN SAVE A MINIMUM OF £5 AND A MAXIMUM OF £150 PER MONTH.

I wish to save £   per month.

Please insert an X in the appropriate box.

	Yes	No
Have you a record of ill-health?	☐	☐
Have you attended hospital or clinic in the last 2 years?	☐	☐
Have you had an AIDS blood test?	☐	☐
Do you take part in any dangerous activities?	☐	☐

If you have answered "Yes" to any of the above, please give details.

....

....

Signature ....   Date ....

MOORE AND BEEVERS LTD
PAINTERS AND DECORATORS

JOB NO ....

JOB ....

....

AT ....

....

FOR ....

ACTION

MATERIALS	COST
	£

Estimated time ....

Employee's name ....

Works No ....

Date ....

GLEDHILL FIRTH PLC

Lanes Industrial Estate
NOTTINGHAM NG7 8ML

PURCHASE ORDER

To:

Order No ....

Date ....

Ref ....

Please deliver to:

Name .... Dept ....

Code No	No	Description	Price each

SIGNED BY ....

PANESEAL LTD
West Lane, BATH, AVON, BA3 4RT

HOME IMPROVEMENT CONTRACT

Name ....

Address ....

....

....

Please install at the above address PANESEAL as listed below at a total cost of

£

		Any special arrangements
Cash Price	£	
VAT	£	
Total Price	£	
Deposit	£	
Balance	£	

Signature of Purchaser ....

Date ....

Location	Description	Overall Size (mm) Width Height

Installation may take more than one day.

Delivery will be in .... to .... weeks.

P·R·O·P·E·T
PROTECTION FOR YOUR PET

APPLICATION FORM

* Please delete as appropriate

Name (Mr/Mrs/Miss/Ms)* ....

Address – No and Road ....

       Town ....

       County ....

       Postcode ....

Tel No .... STD ....

Type of pet   Cat/Dog/Other*   Age ....

Pet's name .... Male/Female*

Please give details of veterinary treatment within the last 12 months.

....

....

....

....

Protection required – please insert X in box.

Pearl ☐   Silver ☐   Platinum ☐

Annual premium £.......................
£26.75 (Pearl) £42.75 (Silver) £53.00 (Platinum)

Payment by Cheque/Access/Visa*

Credit Card No ....

Signature ....

Date ....

SILVER INSURANCE
67 Stanley Road, Blackpool, PR4 6LY

Please send me details of Silver Car Insurance

Full name (Mr/Mrs/Miss/Ms)* ....

Address ....

....

....

Postcode ....

Date of Birth   /   /

Occupation ....

Car Make ....   Model ....

Saloon/Estate/Hatchback*

Reg no ....   Year ....

CC ....   Value ....

Cover required (please enter X in appropriate box)

Comprehensive ☐

Third party, fire and theft ☐

Third party ☐

Will anyone aged 25 or under drive the car? ....

I have been driving for .... years and at present have a ....
No Claims Discount.

I have/have not* been convicted of a driving offence within the last 5 years.

Signature ....   Date ....
*Please delete as applicable

OZONE TOURS LIMITED

Booking Form

Departure date ....

From   Gatwick/Manchester/Birmingham/Luton *

To ....

Destination ....   Resort ....

Hotel ....   No of nights ....

FORENAME(S)	SURNAME	BOARD	ROOM

S-single   TW-twin   D-double   F-family
BB-bed & breakfast   HB-half board   FB-full board

INSURANCE REQUIRED   Yes/No *

PAYMENT BY CREDIT CARD   Access/Visa/Other *

Please charge £................................ to my credit card account

Card number   ☐☐☐☐ ☐☐☐☐ ☐☐☐☐ ☐☐☐☐ ☐☐

Cardholder's name ....

Address ....

....

....

....

Please delete as applicable

STUDENT SUBJECT RECORD

Please complete the form for the subjects to be studied until the end of this school year.

NAME ....

FORM ....

SCHOOL ....

Subject Title	Examining Board	Paper

Signature ....

Home Address ....

....

....

....

Careers Officer ....

Date ....

TOP-PLUS SUPPLIES

Invoice to:

Delivery Note

Deliver to:

Details

Delivery: Van Route ....   No ....

Product No	Description	Quantity	Reference

Date ....

ORDER FORM

I enclose a cheque/postal order * for £
(Cheques and postal orders should be made payable to Rags Fashions)

Name (Mr/Mrs/Miss) * ....

Address ....

....

....

....

Postcode ....

Order Code	Description	Size	Quantity	Price £	Sub-total £
				Total £	

ALL PRICES INCLUSIVE OF VAT AND POSTAGE/PACKING

SIGNED .... DATE ....

Delete as applicable

Wildlife

E N T R Y   F O R M

The entry fee of £1 per photograph for adults and 50p per photograph for children should accompany this form. Please make cheques payable to NATURE IN THE REGIONS. Up to 3 photographs can be entered in each category. Please enter Animal/Plant/Habitat in the Category column and enter an X in the appropriate place.

ADULT SECTION					
CATEGORY	NO	SLIDE	PRINT	COLOUR	MONOCHROME

Name _____

Address _____

_____

Home Telephone Number _____

CHILD SECTION					
CATEGORY	NO	SLIDE	PRINT	COLOUR	MONOCHROME

Name _____

Address _____

_____

Home Telephone Number _____ Age _____

A cheque is enclosed for £